THERE'S A LITTLE SPOT I KNOW

By

JIM BABCOCK

Published 1985 by
The Sacramento Bee
Second Printing 1986

Jim Babcock

This book is a collection of photographs and drawings created by Jim Babcock for The Sacramento Bee under the title, "There's A Little Spot I Know". Featured are 123 of Jim's best of the series that he researched, rode to on his motorcycle with his wife, photographed, wrote the copy, drew the map and did the layout.

In addition to this collection, Jim created many other features for The Sacramento Bee during his 33½ years of service. He joined The Bee in 1950 and started a strip called "Buzzing Around Superior California". The Fresno and Modesto Bees started carrying the strip also and it ran for 16 years.

A 25 year Bee feature, "Sportoons", was created by Jim in 1951. Other reader favorites by Babcock, included California highlights under the titles, "Meet Your Counties", "Your Town", "State Parks", and a collection of illustrated historical facts, " California Nuggets".

Jim Babcock retired from The Bee in 1984. He still continues, however, to occasionally visit little places he knows and supplies them to The Bee. . . perhaps someday, enough to make the second volume in this series.

INTRODUCTION

From Sacramento the
roads and highways head out
in all directions leading to
many interesting and enjoyable
places to see and visit.

This book is a compilation
of some of those spots
that can take from a couple
of hours to several days to complete.

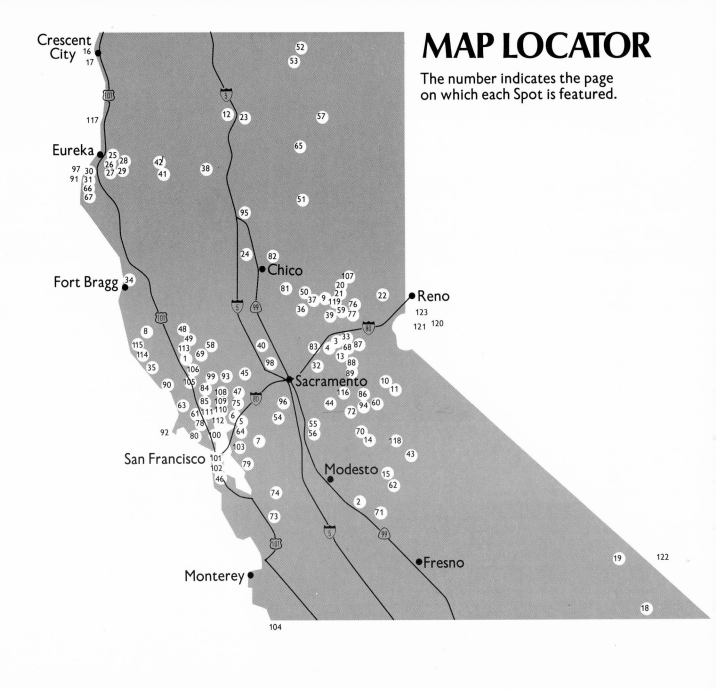

MAP LOCATOR

The number indicates the page
on which each Spot is featured.

THERE'S A LITTLE SPOT I KNOW

A
Asti - Small Catholic church
Atwater - Castle Air Force Base Museum
Auburn/Foresthill Road - Stage Horse Memorial
Auburn - Old Town Post Office

B
Benicia - First Military Hospital built in Far West
Benicia - Third State Capital
Black Diamond Mines Regional Preserve
Boonville

C
Camptonville Monument
Caples Lake
Carson Pass - Unknown Pioneer
Castle Crags State Park
Coloma - Gold Discovery Site
Columbia State Park
Coulterville - Original Chinese structure
Crescent City Lighthouse
Crescent City - St. George Reef Lighthouse

D
Death Valley - Harmony Borax Works
Death Valley - Scotty's Castle
Downieville - Cannon
Downieville - Hanging Scaffold
Downieville - Man made water falls
Dunsmuir - Railroad Park

E
Elk Creek - Grindstone Reservation Roundhouse
Eureka - Carson Mansion
Eureka - Dolos
Eureka - Donkey Engine
Eureka - Ft. Humboldt
Eureka - Large copper statue - "The Fisherman"

F
Ferndale - Gumdrop Cypress Trees/Berding Home
Ferndale - Humboldt County Fairground/
    Cape Mendocino lighthouse replica
Folsom Lake - Peninsula State Park Campground
Forest Hill - Church Bell
Fort Bragg - Lumber/Logging Museum
Fort Ross - State Historic Park
French Corral - Covered Bridge
French Corral - Wells Fargo Express
French Gulch - Hotel

G
Grass Valley - North Star Power House
Grimes/Colusa - Little Brick Shrine

H
41 Hayfork - Bridge Gulch
42 Hayfork - Little Log Cabin School
43 Hetch Hetchy Reservoir

I
44 Ione - Preston Castle

K
45 Knoxville - Quicksilver Mine Headquarters

L
46 Lake Merced - Senator Broderick/
    Chief Justice Terry Duel Site
47 Lake Solano - County Park
48 Lakeport - Blue Steeple Gallery
49 Lakeport - Lake County Court House
50 La Porte
51 Lassen Volcanic National Park - Hot Rock
52 Lava Beds National Monument - Caves
53 Lava Beds National Monument Indian Battle Site
54 Locke - Community Hall/School Building
55 Lodi - Micki Grove Park/
    San Joaquin County Historical Museum
56 Lodi - Mission Arch
57 Lookout - Town
58 Lower Lake - Lake County's First Jail

M
59 Malakoff Diggins State Historical Park
60 Markleeville - Grover Hot Springs
61 Marin French Cheese Company
62 Mariposa County Court House
63 Marshall - Small town on Tomales Bay
64 Martinez - John Muir Home
65 McArthur Burney Falls St. Park
66 Mendocino Temple House
67 Mendocino - Town
68 Michigan Bluff
69 Middletown - 1st white settlers home in Lake County
70 Moaning Cavern
71 Modesto - Millers Horse and Buggy Ranch
72 Mokelumne Hill - Old Church
73 Morgan Hill - Wagons to Wings Relic Collection
74 Mount Hamilton - Lick Observatory

N
75 Napa County Landmark - Old Man Rock Formation
76 Nevada City - Hydraulic Mining Market
77 Nevada City - Indian Medicine Stone
78 Novato - City Hall

O
79 Oakland - Lake Merritt
80 Olema - Earthquake Trail
81 Oroville - Historical House Museum

P
82 Paradise - Honey Run Covered Bridge
83 Penryn - Granite Quarry Park
84 Petaluma - Adobe State Historic Park
85 Petaluma - Iron-front Buildings
86 Pine Grove - Indian Grinding Rock
    State Historical Park
87 Placer Big Tree Grove
88 Placerville - Gold Bug Mine
89 Placerville Soda Works
90 Point Arena Lighthouse
91 Point Cabrillo Lighthouse
92 Point Reys Light Station
93 Pope Valley - Litto, The Hub Cap King

R
94 Railroad Flat - Old Country Store
95 Red Bluff - Wm B. Ide Historical Monument
96 Rio Vista - 3 delta ferries
97 Russian Gulch State Park - Devil's Punch Bowl

S
98 Sacramento River - Monument Bend
99 St. Helena - Robert Louis Stevenson Museum
100 San Francisco - Dutch-style windmill/
    Golden Gate Park
101 San Francisco - Fort Point
102 San Francisco - Japanese Tea Garden/
    Golden Gate Park
103 San Pablo Bay - East Brother Lighthouse
104 San Simeon State Historical Monument/
    Hearst Castle
105 Santa Rosa - Fountain Grove Colony
    Round Red Barn
106 Santa Rosa - Luther Burbank Home
107 Sierra City - Kentucky Gold Mine
108 Sonoma Cheese Factory
109 Sonoma - General Vallejo's Home
110 Sonoma - Mountain Cemetary
111 Sonoma Plaza
112 Sonoma - Scene of Historical Bear Flag Revolt
113 Squaw Rock - Hopland
114 Stewarts Point - Kashia Indian Reservation
    Redwood Roundhouse
115 Stewarts Point - General Store
116 Sutter Creek Foundry

T
117 Trinidad - Lighthouse and Harbour
118 Tuolumne - Indian Roundhouses

W
119 Washington - Old Gold Mine Town

Nevada
120 Fort Churchill State Park
121 Genoa Station -
    First permanent settlement in Nevada
122 Rhyolite - Bottle House
123 Virginia City

There's A Little Spot I Know

by

Jim Babcock

Possibly someone should pray to God to save the Little Church of Asti before it crumbles and falls.

The small Catholic church has long been a landmark along Highway 101. It is located 3 miles south of Cloverdale.

In recent years, a modern church has been built a short distance away, but the new one doesn't hold an altar candle to the quaint little shingled church which resembles a wine cask.

Bypassed by the freeway and time, the small church of Our Lady of Carmel sits beside the old highway, a part of yesterday and, we hope, tomorrow.

There's A Little Spot I Know

by

Jim Babcock

A
SALUTE
TO THE
PAST —
J. babcock

It was a cold, damp and foggy day when I visited the Castle Air Museum in Atwater. As I stood under a dripping wing I was transported back in time to 1944-45 when war birds such as those displayed here went forth each day to do battle with the enemy.

The distinct sounds of B-17s coughing, then sputtering to life in early dawn . . . muffled voices of tired but brave young men boarding their planes . . . squealing brakes ridden hard to hold taxi position . . . the roar of full power as the bomb-laden Forts staggered into the air to join up with other groups for another day of living or dying.

The memory faded as quickly as it appeared — and maybe that's best.

The haunting sounds and aircraft of that period have all but disappeared, but thanks to the Air Force's Heritage Program and a group of dedicated enthusiasts in the Atwater-Merced area, the 23 vintage aircraft and museum are open to the public for their enjoyment.

Among the many fine restored aircraft are a B-17 Flying Fortress, B-25 Mitchell, B-26 Marauder, B-29 Superfortress, B-50 Superfortress, plus a huge delta-wing, the British B-2 Vulcan jet. Presently 22 other military aircraft are being restored for future display.

The indoor exhibit features uniforms, photos, personal equipment, a restaurant and a gift shop. The museum is open each day except for major holidays.

File a flight plan and enjoy a flight to yesterday. While there, ask about the haunted plane!

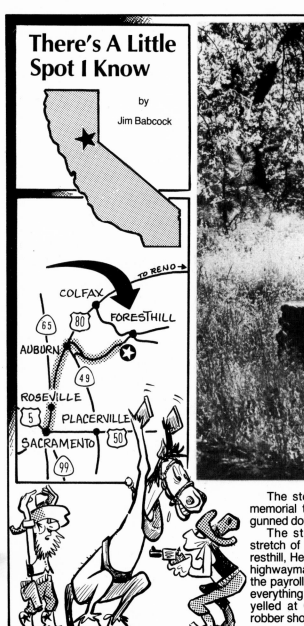

There's A Little Spot I Know

by

Jim Babcock

OLD JOE, A STAGE HORSE, WAS SHOT
BY A STAGE ROBBER, JULY 3, 1901.
HENRY CROCKET WAS STAGE DRIVER,
AND WHEN ORDERED TO STOP, SAID,
"YOU ARE ONLY FOOLING." AT THAT
OLD JOE WAS SHOT AND THE STAGE
ROBBED. THE ROBBER TURNED OUT
TO BE HENRY WISE AND WAS NEVER
HEARD OF AGAIN.

ERECTED BY
AUBURN PARLOR #59
N.S.G.W

The stone marker was placed as a memorial to a four-footed Western hero gunned down in 1901.

The story goes that on the lonely stretch of road between Auburn and Foresthill, Henry Crockett was stopped by a highwayman and ordered to throw down the payroll. Henry, not seeming to believe everything that he heard or saw refused, yelled at Old Joe to giddup. Then the robber shot Old Joe.

The robber escaped but Old Joe was laid to rest on the spot.

Later the N.S.G.W. erected the marker and stone to commemorate the passing of Old Joe.

Locating the marker and sign requires a bit of looking as you motor up from Auburn to Foresthill, but if you keep a sharp eye out, soon after passing Monte Verdi you will be rewarded by the sign that tells it all.

There's A Little Spot I Know

by

Jim Babcock

Auburn's post office in "old town" is not the biggest, smallest, or maybe even the quaintest, but it does have one outstanding feature that gives it a stamp of approval no other post office in California has.

It has the distinction of having been in operation longer than any other post office in the state.

Old town originally was a tent city that took care of miners' needs, but this section was practically abandoned in 1852. Following a disastrous fire the second stage of what is old town was rebuilt after 1855 — this time with buildings of stone and brick. That is when the old post office was built.

Jutting up in the background of the photo above is a structure that probably is one of the most photographed buildings in California. The firehouse, built in 1891, is another landmark that has stood the test of time.

There's A Little Spot I Know

by
Jim Babcock

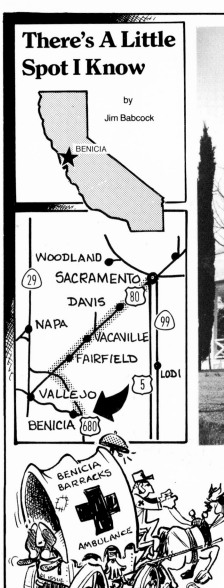

A lone building, the first military hospital built in the Far West, is all that remains of Benicia Barracks, a post that once shared hills northeast of Benicia with the arsenal.

The building, completed in 1856 at a cost of $12,000, was constructed of sandstone blocks with a porch across the front. It served military casualties from Indian uprisings as far away as the Northwest Territory. It contained two wards, kitchen, mess, office, "dead room" (morgue) and a storeroom. During World War II the old hospital building became the post chapel.

It has weathered storms and a fire that wiped out the other post buildings, and now is nearly surrounded by an industrial area.

To find this little spot, take the Benicia Industrial Park turnoff, turn left at first stop sign, then follow the road past the concrete ammunition bunkers. When you pass the National Guard area, start looking to the right for the little hospital.

It stands out like a sore thumb, but don't expect first aid. The hospital closed in 1924.

There's A Little Spot I Know

by

Jim Babcock

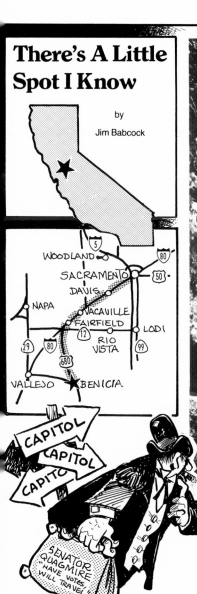

Benicia's most noteworthy and prominent building in the 1850s was the third State Capitol, located on the northwest corner of First and G streets.

The building, built in 1852 and intended to be used as the City Hall, was offered to the state and served as the Capitol from Feb. 4, 1853, until Feb. 25, 1854. Three days later the "Capitol on wheels" departed for Sacramento.

Since its early days of glory the building has served as courthouse, school, library, church, City Hall and theater; maybe not in that order, but always with distinction.

In 1949, it was deeded to the state and underwent a $230,000 restoration to its former Grecian Temple look. That is $200,-000 more than it originally cost. The building, now a State Historical Monument, is open to the public.

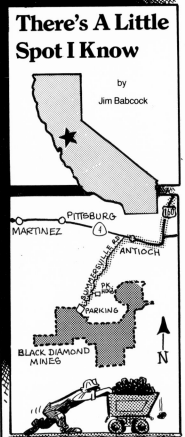

There's A Little Spot I Know

by

Jim Babcock

Nortonville, Sommersville, Stewartville, West Hartley and Judsonville have completely disappeared with time, but the mine shafts and the lonely little Rose Hill cemetery are a reminder of the early miners and their families who toiled and died here. From the 1860s until 1902, a low-grade coal was mined, later the Sommersville mine produced sand for making glass until 1949. The Black Diamond Mines Regional Preserve has numerous botanical, geological and wildlife resources to enjoy. To fully enjoy the park, take a guided weekend tour which includes a walking trip to and through some of the mine sites. Reservations may be made by calling 757-2620 on weekends between 10:30 and 11:30 a.m. From Sacramento, take river road 160 to Antioch, turn left on Summersville and continue to Park Headquarters. Picnic tables are located near the parking lot.

There's A Little Spot I Know

by

Jim Babcock

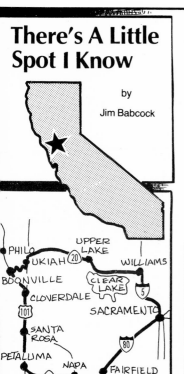

If you think you may have taken the wrong turnoff and ended up in a place where people look quite normal but speak a strange language, fret not.

The "harpins" (words) on the Coffee Shop sign and the name on the "teleef'n" (telephone) booth indicate that you are passing through the town of Boonville, where Boont-ling originated in the late 1800s and the early 1900s.

This little spot is where early Boonters delighted in "sharkin' kimeys" (stumping visitors) from the "bright lights" (San Francisco) or other nearby towns such as "Clerdal" (Cloverdale) or "Uke" (Ukiah).

Boont lingo consists of more than 1,000 words, some "deejy" (bad) and some "plenty bahl" (good), but all related to a happening, a place or a name.

"Zeese" translates to coffee, "Bucky Walters" denotes a pay telephone (named for Walters who had the first telephone in the area) and "Bucky" for the old-time nickel with the Indian head on it.

How do I know the words? I was born in Boonville and my mother and I still get a boot out of recalling Boontling. My mother's grandfather and family came to Boonville in the mid-1850s and she recalls washing dishes in the old Berry Hotel while standing on a box. Her grandmother ran the Missouri House and the hotel across the street — way back when.

The old Berry Hotel has undergone many changes, but it still serves some mighty fine "gorms." J. T.'s store, with the old dance hall on the second floor, stands silent today, but the Bucket of Blood has a new front and still gets its share of "high Kimeys" on Saturday nights.

There's A Little Spot I Know

by

Jim Babcock

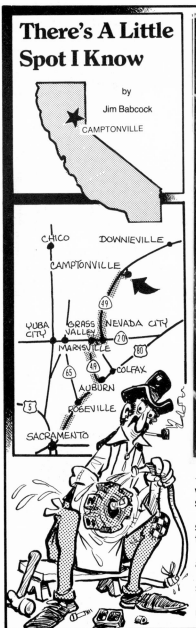

CAMPTONVILLE

CHICO · DOWNIEVILLE
CAMPTONVILLE
YUBA CITY · GRASS VALLEY · NEVADA CITY
MARYSVILLE · 49 · 20
65 · 49 · COLFAX · 80
AUBURN
5 · ROSEVILLE
SACRAMENTO

Monuments honoring two men who helped write the history of the Gold Country repose in a serene setting on the west end of Camptonville.

Seen by those entering the town from the south, the stone markers honor Robert Campton and Lester Allen Pelton.

Campton, a blacksmith who arrived in the area in 1852, had the town named for him.

Pelton, who arrived somewhat later, designed and built the Pelton water wheel.

Power supplied by the Pelton wheel helped run mine machinery, early electric plants and other operations.

Once a stopover for mule trains that plodded up the mountain from Nevada City and Marysville on their way to Downieville, Camptonville retains the charm of yesteryear, thanks in part to the fact that Highway 49 skirts the edge of town.

Most of the town's original buildings were lost in fires, but the quaintness of the small community remains to be enjoyed by visitors. As it has for many years, Camptonville continues to sit quietly, watching today slip into yesterday.

There's A Little Spot I Know

by

Jim Babcock

Caples Lake is one of the many jewels that sparkle in the high Sierra. Once known as Summit lake, Clear Lake, Caples Twin Lakes and Twin Lakes Reservoir, the lake in 1970 was officially named Caples Lake, for the family that settled there in the 1850s.

Close by the lake is an excellent federal campground with 38 sites, complete with rest-rooms. Across the highway is a resort with cabins, small store and boat launching facilities. The lake has six species of trout. They can be found by trolling, bank fishing or radar.

From Sacramento, drive east on Highway 50 to Sly Park and take the recently paved road that comes out on Highway 88. From this pont it is 13 miles east to Caples Lake.

There's A Little Spot I Know

by
Jim Babcock

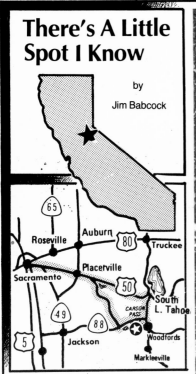

High atop the Sierra a short distance from Carson Pass is the grave of an unknown pioneer whose stone-mounted marker reminds us of the area's early settlers.

A bronze marker bears these words: "The Unknown Pioneer, 1849. Here rests one whose name is known only to our creator. He was one of the valiant calvalcade who brought honor and stability to the character of California. Faith in God . . . Faith in themselves. . . Faith in their fellowmen. . . . Rever-ently dedicated Aug. 27, 1950 by the Odd Fellows of California and assisted by their brothers of Nevada."

Nearby is the old Immigrant Trail that threaded its way over Carson Pass. Today, Highway 88 climbs out of the heated valley and passes through the pine forest, running along many beautiful lakes and twisting through Carson Pass before moving down the eastern side of the Sierra. What once was a two-week trip now takes two hours to drive.

There's A Little Spot I Know

by
Jim Babcock

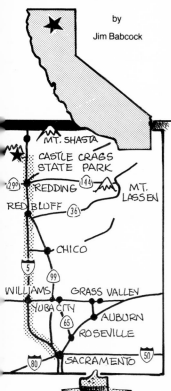

Castle Crags is not a little spot.

It is, to be more exact, a mighty big spot — one that is sharply etched against the blue sky, thrusting glacial rock walls upward more than 4,000 feet above the valley floor.

Castle Crags State Park, 43 miles north of Redding on Highway 5, nestles against the base of the towering domes. For a really good show, take the 1½-lane road that snakes its way for a mile from within the park to Vista.Point, where visitors enjoy a view of the Grey Rocks mountain range to the southwest, Castle Crags to the west and Mount Shasta to the north. From Vista Point a trail leads to the base of lower promontories of the domes. This trail rises 2,000 feet and entails a 5½-mile hike.

Those planning a visit should bring clothing for warm days, cool nights and sometimes-wet afternoons. A camera is a must to record the awe-inspiring views, but there is no guarantee that an airplane, like the one at lower right in the photo above, will fly into your picture.

There's A Little Spot I Know

by
Jim Babcock

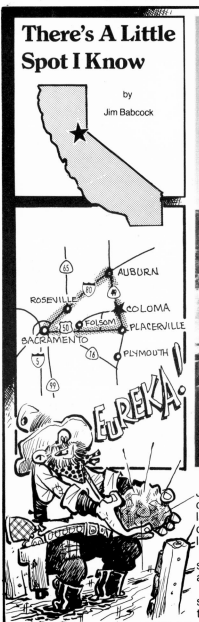

Just imagine, if Capt. John Sutter and James Marshall hadn't blabbed about the discovery of gold, California might still be isolated, known only for its tall redwoods, foggy coastline, 21 missions, a Russian Fort and a lack of water in the south.

When Marshall found gold at the Coloma site, the world beat a path to the golden gate and almost knocked it off its hinges.

From 1849 on, California boomed with gold seekers and gold diggers of all types, seeking their fortune by hook or crook.

Some of the newcomers moved on, but most stayed on to become the nucleus of what we loosely refer to as "native Californians."

Coloma today is a state park, honoring James Marshall.

Within the park boundaries are a replica of the mill, the Marshall cabin and numerous old stores and buildings dating back to 1849.

Pack a picnic, invite friends and spend an interesting day at the spot where it all happened.

There's A Little Spot I Know

by

Jim Babcock

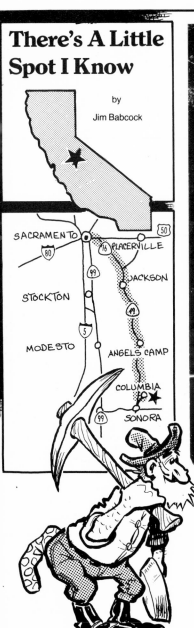

Columbia is considered the best-preserved gold-mining town in the United States and a living museum of California's past.

After two disastrous fires in the early 1850s, Columbia was rebuilt of brick to stand the test of fire, weather and time.

Most of the town is a State Park, so visitors can walk the main street without worrying about being knocked down by an automobile. On the other hand, visitors might be alert for horse-drawn buggies, stagecoaches and ornery old miners.

Columbia, a short distance from Sonora, once was the second-largest city in California, with a population of 10,000 gold seekers, four banks, eight hotels, 40 saloons, 53 stores, 150 gambling dens — and three churches. That should tell you something.

During the great gold rush, Columbia saw $87 million ripped from its soil in one way or another until the supply was depleted.

Thank you, California, for not allowing a valuable and historical piece of our past to vanish into dust.

There's A Little Spot I Know

by

Jim Babcock

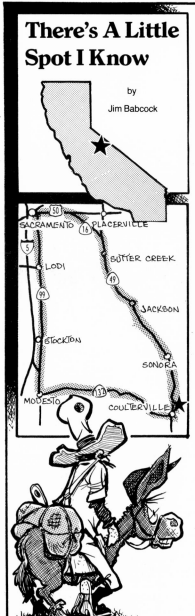

San Francisco may have the largest Chinatown in the United States, but Coulterville's could be the smallest.

Coulterville, located about midway between Sonora and Mariposa on Highway 49, started out as a trading post and soon thereafter developed into a mining town.

As did many ethnic groups of the Gold Rush period, the Chinese developed their own community, this time on the outskirts of Coulterville.

Numerous fires ravaged the town and only a few of the original buildings were unscathed. Today only two of Coulterville Chinatown's structures stand.

Most noteworthy is the Sun Sun Wo Merchandise store which was built of adobe, with rough wood siding and a tin roof.

Today, the small, weatherbeaten structure rests quietly on the east side of town, sitting patiently for the numerous tourists who whip out a camera and endeavor to record a piece of history before it fades away into yesterday.

There's A Little Spot I Know

by

Jim Babcock

The Crescent City light station, considered one of the finest examples of 1850s lighthouse architecture in Northern California, is joined to the mainland during low tide by a narrow strip of rocky beach.

From the stone foundation to the black lantern room 75 feet above sea level, the station is an excellent example of lighthouse construction. Massive tidal waves have hurled rock, gravel and seaweed onto the roof and high winds and storms have shattered windows, but the station, built in 1856, remains intact.

To guide ships, the fourth-order lens emitted a steady white beam plus a brilliant flash every 90 seconds to guide ships. The Coast Guard automated the station in 1953 and leased it to the Del Norte County Historical Society as a museum. Although open to the public, the station may be visited only at low tide.

'Tis rumored that on dark and stormy nights the clump of heavy sea boots may be heard, first climbing the stairs to the lantern room, then disappearing into the crashing wave sounds. Until proven otherwise, I'll believe the story.

There's A Little Spot I Know

by

Jim Babcock

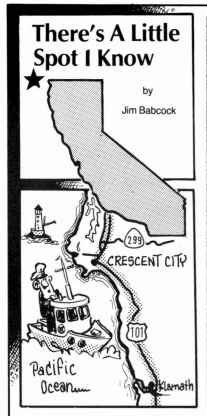

Emerging from the churning green sea like a monster from the depths, the St. George Reef Lighthouse stares out through the stormiest nights and the foggiest days, but not one glimmer of light shines from its black lantern room.

Built over a period of 10 years, the lighthouse is anchored firmly to Northwest Seal Rock, 6 miles west of Crescent City, in treacherous waters that have claimed many lives and ships.

The lighthouse is this country's tallest, largest and was the most costly to build. When weather permitted, supplies, keepers and boats were hoisted onto the landing by a 90-foot boom. Three Coast Guardsmen were lost in 1951 when a huge sleeper wave flipped their boat while it was on the boom.

The lighthouse base consisted of an oval foundation 70 feet high and 68 feet long that was constructed of dovetailed, 2½-ton stone blocks quarried near Eureka. The base contains numerous rooms and a 120,000-gallon cistern. The pyramidal tower rises 64 feet from the top of the base. Total cost was $704,000.

The structure used 175,260 cubic feet of granite, 1,439 tons of sand, 335 tons of brick and 272 tons of gravel. Many workers were injured and one rigger was killed during construction.

On Oct. 20, 1892, both the light and fog whistle began operation and continued until May 13, 1975, when the colors came down, the doors were padlocked and the crew was removed. The lighthouse is intact. The curtain around its Fresnel lens was drawn and the giant among light houses was retired — replaced by a large navigational buoy that is moored nearby.

The lighthouse may be viewed from numerous places along the Del Norte coast and as far north as Brookings, Ore. To see and photograph America's greatest lighthouse from the coast, take along binoculars and a camera with a long telephoto lens.

There's A Little Spot I Know

by
Jim Babcock

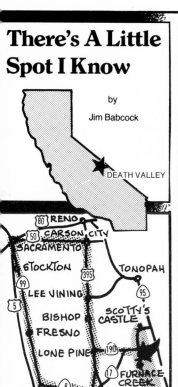

THE 20 MULE TEAM WAGON TRAIN REQUIRED 10 DAYS TO TRAVEL 165 MILES AND PULLED A TOTAL OF 36½ TONS.

The quest for riches leads miners into many strange places, but nothing compares with the sizzling desert heat that man and beast worked in to extract borax from Death Valley.

Not much stands of the old Harmony Borax Works in Death Valley, the site where Aaron Winters discovered borax in 1881.

Shortly after the discovery Winters sold his holdings to W.T. Coleman of San Francisco.

Coleman used Chinese laborers to gather the raw material, called "cotton ball," and transport it to a small plant he built near Furnace Creek for processing. The pure borax then was carried by specially designed wagons to the railhead at Mojave for shipment to Los Angeles. It was for these shipments that the famous 20-mule-team wagon trains, pulled by 18 mules and two lead horses, were developed.

Operations at Harmony Borax Works ceased in 1889 after a sharp drop in the price of borax.

When you plan your visit, save summertime for a trip to the coast or high mountains because you could hit a time when the temperature is 120 degrees in the shade at Death Valley.

There's A Little Spot I Know

by

Jim Babcock

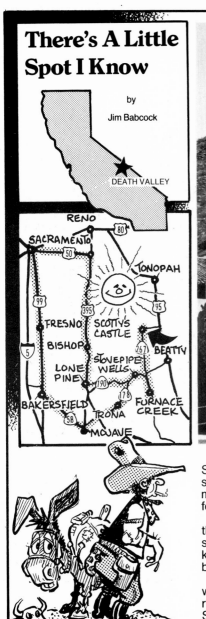

DEATH VALLEY

Albert Johnson and his friend Death Valley Scotty took 7 years to construct a castle that stands at the northern end of Death Valley. The magnificent structure defies most explanations for its being except that it was a challenge.

Death Valley Ranch had 1,500 acres of land that would hardly support lizards, but with Johnson's backing and Scotty's ingenuity and knowledge of the desert the castle grew and blossomed like a cactus.

When the project began in 1922, all materials were trucked in over dirt roads, either from a railhead 28 miles away or from Goldfield, Nev. Spring water turned a Pelton waterwheel to generate electricity. The wheel later was replaced by a diesel-powered unit.

The castle, an oasis in the high desert country (3,000 ft.), was never considered a working ranch, but more of a retreat for Johnson and his friends.

Johnson died in 1948, and Scotty lived at the ranch until his death in 1954. The U.S. government bought the ranch in 1970 and made it part of Death Valley National Monument.

The castle is open to the public throughout the year, but the ideal time to visit is November through April to avoid the hot desert heat of midsummer.

There's A Little Spot I Know

by
Jim Babcock

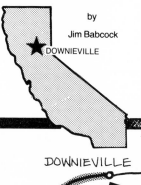

DOWNIEVILLE

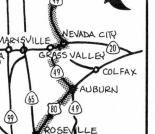

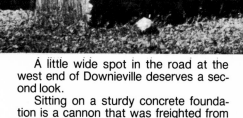

A little wide spot in the road at the west end of Downieville deserves a second look.

Sitting on a sturdy concrete foundation is a cannon that was freighted from San Francisco by horse and wagon and arrived on July 1, 1862.

The old 12-pounder was used to celebrate various fetes during the Gold Rush days. Its loud report was described as "peaceful thunder at the portals."

But on May 27, 1863 tragedy struck during the celebration of the supposed winning of the Battle of Vicksburg by the Union Army.

Lt. M.M. Knox and 2nd Lt. William A. Donalson of Company K, 6th Regiment of the California Volunteers, were killed when the cannon discharged during loading. Knox was blown over the steep embankment, almost to the river far below. His final words were, "I had a pretty hard ride down here, boys. Well, I don't care, Vicksburg was taken."

Ironically, the report which brought on the celebration was premature. Vicksburg fell to the Union Army the following July.

There's A Little Spot I Know

by

Jim Babcock

DOWNIEVILLE

The signs to the right of the picture have nothing to do with the old hanging scaffold, but could be a deterrent to committing a violent crime in Sierra County.

Downieville had a colorful and gutsy past during the Gold Rush era, including the hanging of a woman for stabbing a miner to death in 1851. Controversy continues as to whether the hanging took place on a bridge or on a makeshift gallows, but it is certain that this was the first woman to meet her maker in this manner in California. The gal-lows that stands in the shadow of the Courthouse was not involved. It was built in 1857. The last execution in the county was in 1885.

From Sacramento, take Highway 80 to Auburn, pick up Highway 49 and continue to Downieville. The gallows is difficult to see because it is painted deep green and blends in with the tree foliage. The signs, incidentally, are for a one-way street exit around the courthouse, but could mean the same thing for the old gallows.

There's A Little Spot I Know

by
Jim Babcock

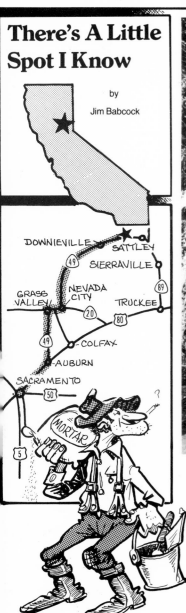

Amusement parks and concrete cities may offer variations of man-made waterfalls, but they are a mere drop in the bucket compared to Mother Nature's display of water over the rocks at this little spot in the High Sierra.

Located on Highway 49 east of Downieville, the gushing waterfall invites the motorist to stop, park and marvel at the streams of water that seem to flow from the embankment.

A small monument was built by Peter A. "Pete" Lavezolla in his spare time. Pete served the area as a foreman for the state Highway Department.

The Native Sons of the Golden West, Downieville Parlor 92, erected a small bronze plaque dedicated to Pete, who built the fountain for the enjoyment of passersby.

To see the best display, try to make the trip while the icy waters from melting snow still tumble over the rocks like liquid silver.

There's A Little Spot I Know

by
Jim Babcock

DUNSMUIR
SHASTA LAKE
REDDING
RED BLUFF
CHICO
YUBA CITY
MARYSVILLE
99
ROSEVILLE
WOODLAND
50
SACRAMENTO
80

Whether you come to look or to dine, you're in for a delightful experience that you'll savor for a long time.

Going to Railroad Park, one mile south of Dunsmuir, is like taking a journey back to the days of gas-lit dining cars, steam locomotives and red cabooses. In addition, there's a view of Castle Crags that is awe-inspiring.

The lounge is a rail buff's delight. Above the bar is a hand-built scale model of the "Cascade," which ran from San Francisco to Portland, as well as antique hand tools, lamps and other memorabilia.

On a siding sits a Willamette Shay, a gear-driven logging engine, a wooden snowplow, a flanger, a caboose and a restored water tower to add to the authenticity of the setting. Adjoining the Railroad Park is a campground for the R.V enthusiasts and tent campers. It all adds up to a real "Whistle Stop."

There's A Little Spot I Know

by
Jim Babcock

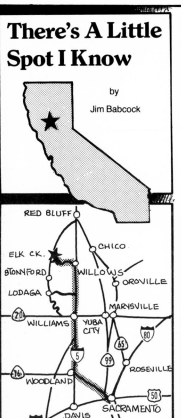

RED BLUFF
ELK CK.
CHICO
STONYFORD
WILLOWS
OROVILLE
LODAGA
MARYSVILLE
20
WILLIAMS
YUBA CITY
65
80
5
99
ROSEVILLE
16
WOODLAND
50
80
DAVIS
SACRAMENTO

Roundhouses, looking like huge mushrooms emerging from the earth, played an important part in the culture of the North American Indians.

The structures were built partly below ground, were banked with dirt and had only one entrance. The dark interior was used for meetings, religious rituals, celebrations, dances and tribal affairs. You might say the roundhouses were a kind of early convention center.

Nearing the 100-year mark, the Grindstone Reservation roundhouse west of Willows is one of few left standing in California.

Visit a roundhouse and you'll come away with a better understanding of a culture that dates back 1,000 years to a time when the original round kivas dotted the Southwest.

If you visit this little spot, please keep in mind that you are a guest on the reservation and accept the hospitality graciously.

There's A Little Spot I Know

by
Jim Babcock

ARCATA
REDDING
299
EUREKA
RED BLUFF
101
5
CHICO
WILLIAMS
20
UKIAH
WOODLAND
ROSEVILLE
SANTA ROSA
50
SACRAMENTO
NOVATO
80
VALLEJO

George Eastman of Kodak fame would rub his hands in glee if he could see the miles and miles of film shot of the Carson Mansion in Eureka.

The mansion, on Second Street, is one of the best examples of Victorian gothic residential architecture in America. You could say that William Carson pulled out all the stops when he built this monument.

Bristling with gingerbread, ornate cupolas and fancy carvings, the mansion was constructed of rich, clear-grained redwood. Three stories tall, with a lordly tower to oversee the Humboldt Bay, 18 rooms and a land-scaped surrounding this is the show-piece of Northern California.

The mansion was built in 1884. Carson lived in it until his death in 1912. His family lived there until it was sold in 1950 to a private club.

There's A Little Spot I Know

by
Jim Babcock

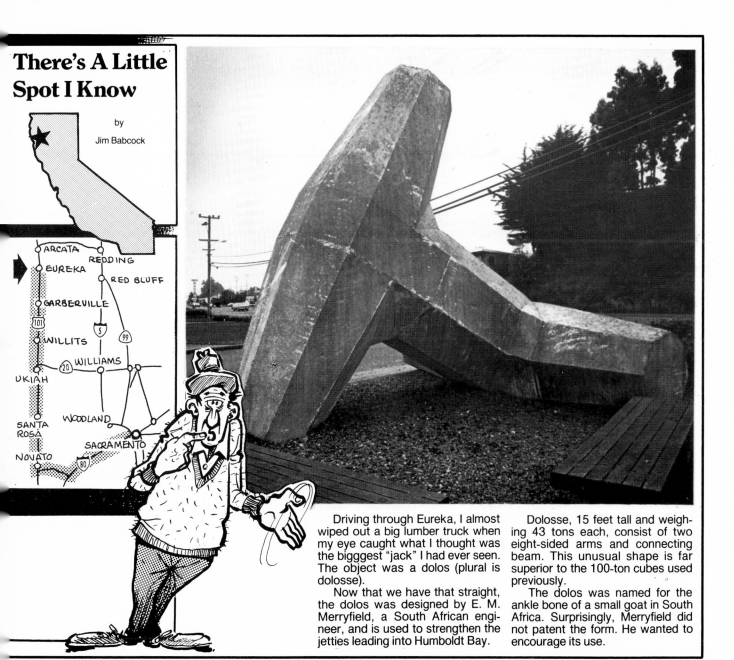

Driving through Eureka, I almost wiped out a big lumber truck when my eye caught what I thought was the bigggest "jack" I had ever seen. The object was a dolos (plural is dolosse).

Now that we have that straight, the dolos was designed by E. M. Merryfield, a South African engineer, and is used to strengthen the jetties leading into Humboldt Bay.

Dolosse, 15 feet tall and weighing 43 tons each, consist of two eight-sided arms and connecting beam. This unusual shape is far superior to the 100-ton cubes used previously.

The dolos was named for the ankle bone of a small goat in South Africa. Surprisingly, Merryfield did not patent the form. He wanted to encourage its use.

26

There's A Little Spot I Know

by
Jim Babcock

If you don't know a donkey engine from a diesel, this is one spot you shouldn't miss.

Located next to Fort Humboldt in Eureka is a very interesting and educational exhibit of early day logging equipment that was used for dragging, hi-flying and transporting the huge redwood logs to the mills.

The logging exhibit has walkways with designated signs that lead the visitor through the whole operation from the fallen timber to the greased ways to the donkey engines that snaked the logs up and down the canyons on their way to the mills.

While there, be sure to visit Fort Humboldt, where Ulysses S. Grant served as a captain in 1853.

Grant left the Army soon after, but went back in when the Civil War broke out.

There's A Little Spot I Know

by
Jim Babcock

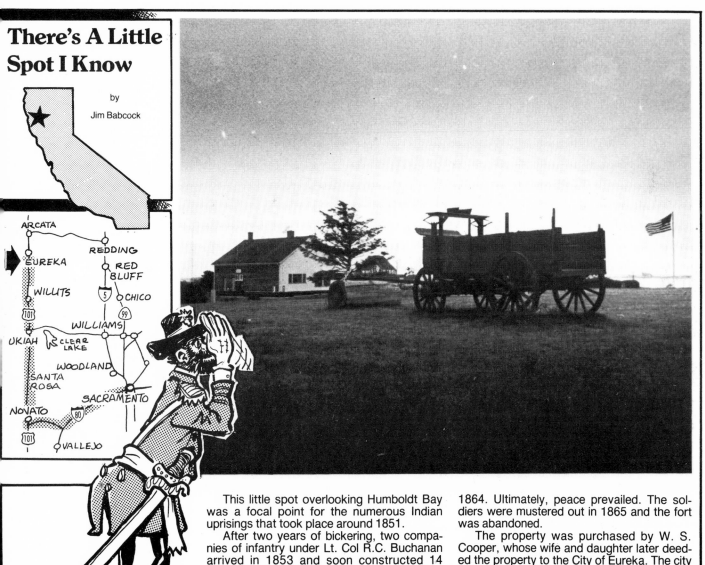

This little spot overlooking Humboldt Bay was a focal point for the numerous Indian uprisings that took place around 1851.

After two years of bickering, two companies of infantry under Lt. Col R.C. Buchanan arrived in 1853 and soon constructed 14 buildings, including a hospital, store, powder magazine, laundry, living quarters and a guard house — all at a cost of $11,664.93.

Skirmishes with the Indians continued until 1864. Ultimately, peace prevailed. The soldiers were mustered out in 1865 and the fort was abandoned.

The property was purchased by W. S. Cooper, whose wife and daughter later deeded the property to the City of Eureka. The city deeded the fort to the State Division of Beaches and Parks in 1955.

The only building left standing is the hospital, which is undergoing restoration.

There's A Little Spot I Know

by
Jim Babcock

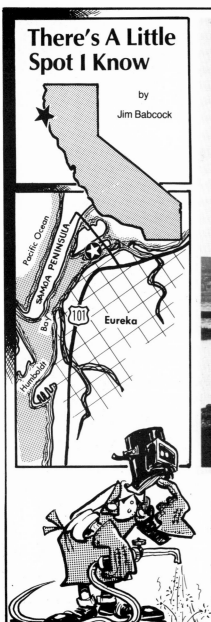

Something new has been added to the Humboldt Bay skyline. It is "The Fisherman," a beautiful large copper statue that graces the Eureka marina just off Woodley island.

A memorial to men lost at sea while pursuing their livelihood, the magnificent statue of a fisherman pulling in his net looms 25 feet above the bay.

It took Eureka artist Dick Crane three years to build the statue. He used 2,000 pounds of 26-ounces-per-square-foot copper sheeting, welding it together to form the fisherman. An additional 5 miles of copper cable was used to construct the net.

Because of natural chemical action of the environment on the copper, the fisherman ultimately will take on a blue-green coloring.

To view the statue and the new marina, take the bridge to Samoa and turn off at Woodley Island.

There's A Little Spot I Know

by
Jim Babcock

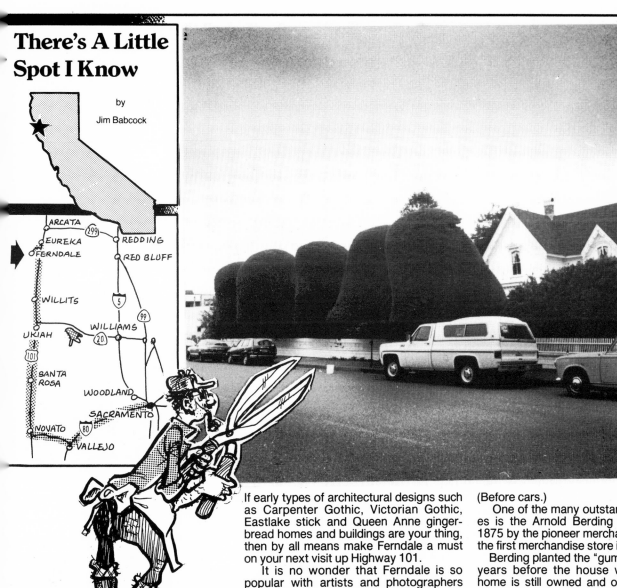

If early types of architectural designs such as Carpenter Gothic, Victorian Gothic, Eastlake stick and Queen Anne gingerbread homes and buildings are your thing, then by all means make Ferndale a must on your next visit up Highway 101.

It is no wonder that Ferndale is so popular with artists and photographers alike. The whole town sparkles with authentic preserved buildings that take you back to the horse 'n' buggy days B.C.

(Before cars.)

One of the many outstanding residences is the Arnold Berding home, built in 1875 by the pioneer merchant who owned the first merchandise store in Ferndale.

Berding planted the "gumdrop trees" 10 years before the house was built. The home is still owned and occupied by his descendants.

The coast cypress trees have always been trimmed once a year.

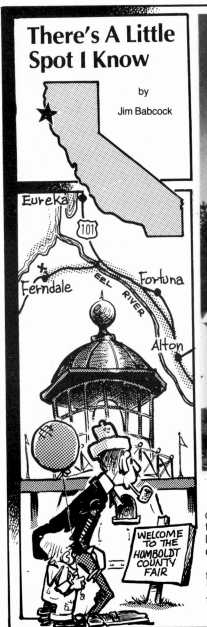

There's A Little Spot I Know

by

Jim Babcock

Most lighthouses perch on prominent points of land that jut out into the ocean, but that isn't the case with the lighthouse at Ferndale. That light is anchored firmly above turnstiles at the entrance to the Humboldt County Fair ground.

Actually, the first order lens was removed from the Cape Mendocino Light Station in 1951 by the Coast Guard when they installed the automatic rotating beacon. Later the auto-matic beacon was taken away and the light-house became dark.

Today the station is closed. A new beacon is nearby and the lighthouse is used only as a reference point by fishermen and other boat-ers. The original Fresnel lens was removed to Ferndale, installed in the replica of the Cape Mendocino station and today serves as a guid-ing light for the Humboldt County Fair goers.

There's A Little Spot I Know

by
Jim Babcock

The park rangers refer to Peninsula Campground as the gem of the state Parks, and rightly so. This little spot, located near the juncture of the North and South Fork of the American River, is also one of the most difficult to reach in the state park system—unless you boat across from the other side of Folsom Lake. Reservations can be made through Ticketron®. The park normally only fills on holidays and weekends.

Peninsula Campground is approximately 60 miles from Sacramento. To reach it, motor to Folsom, take the Green Valley road east a short distance past Browns Ravine, turn left on the Pilot Hill-Salmon Falls Road. Proceed to Pilot Hill and turn left on Rattlesnake Bar Road. A word of caution: The road has a number of sharp turns, is rather narrow and is unpaved in some sections.

At the end of the 7-mile road is remote Peninsula Campground. It has 100 campsites and running water, tables, barbecue pits, flush toilets, a boat ramp and a fantastic view of the lake. Deer, wild turkeys, rabbits and other wildlife abound in the oak-studded park. Anglers may try their luck for bass, trout and crappie. This is also one of the few areas where night-fishing is allowed. If the fish can't see my hook during daylight, how in heck can they find it at night!

There's A Little Spot I Know

by

Jim Babcock

The original St. Joseph's Catholic Church in Foresthill burned in 1952, but the church bell survived and now rests atop a monument on the outskirts of town.

The bell, cast in Sheffield by Naylor Vickers and Co., was shipped from England to Boston in 1862. From this point the bell was loaded on a ship, sailed around the horn to San Francisco and came by boat to Sacramento. The final journey to Foresthill was powered by a six-horse team.

Miners raised $3,500 to pay for the beautiful old bell that rang out to welcome those early Californians to church services.

After the church burned, the Placer County Historical Society erected the monument which stands as a link with our past.

There's A Little Spot I Know

Jim Babcock

No, this isn't Paul Bunyan's home, but it's said he walks by, leading Babe, the blue ox, on his way back to the tall redwoods that thrive in the Fort Bragg area.

The spacious three-story redwood home, with its lovely gardens and numerous exhibits of early day logging equipment, is well worth the stop.

The house was built in 1892 for T. L. Johnson and later became the home of C. R. Johnson, who founded Union Lumber Co. The stately Victorian-style house was the family dwelling until 1912 and it served as the company guest house until 1969.

The museum, located on Main Street in Fort Bragg, is owned by Georgia-Pacific. It's open from 8:30 a.m. to 5:30 p.m. Wednesday through Sunday.

Enjoy stepping back in time for a look at Mendocino County's early lumbering history. It's an enlightening and enjoyable experience!

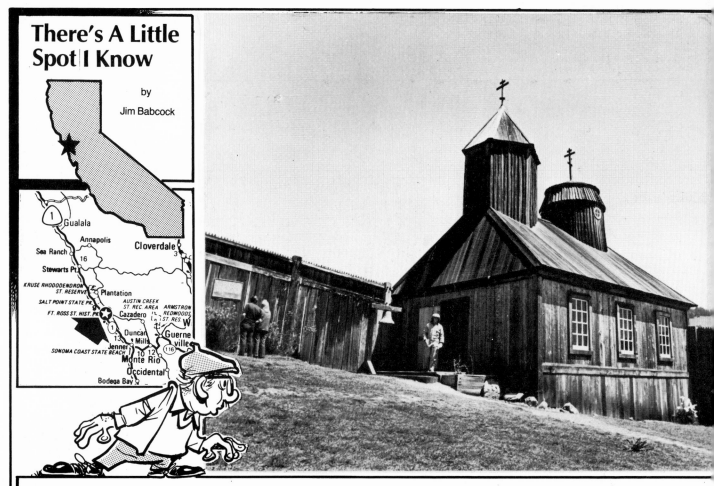

There's A Little Spot I Know

by

Jim Babcock

In 1812, ninety five Russians and forty Aleuts and Kodiak islanders came ashore and built a fort and village on the rugged isolated coast north of San Francisco Bay. The Russians came for many reasons, to hunt sea otter, grow crops and quietly expand holdings along the Pacific coast. Surprisingly, no other countries including the Spanish Americans were even aware of the development of Fort Ross for more than six months.

When the Russians made the decision to leave, the fort was sold to John Sutter of Sacramento in 1841. Once Sutter had removed all valuables, the fort went through a series of owners and in 1903 the site was turned over to the State of California for preservation and restoration as a state historic monument. After extensive rebuilding and reconstructing, Fort Ross looks like it did 170 years ago.

One of the most interesting features is the Orthodox Chapel which has been rebuilt and restored three times. The original Russian bell, completely melted by a tragic fire in 1970, was recast and is on display.

Fort Ross is approximately 145 miles from Sacramento, via Napa, Santa Rosa, Jenner and north on Highway 1 for 13 miles . . .

There's A Little Spot I Know

by

Jim Babcock

The present road to French Corral, Nevada County, leaves Highway 20 midway between Smartville and Rough and Ready.

That paved road twists and turns for five miles before passing close by the longest single-span covered bridge in the nation.

The Bridgeport bridge (Named for a town that once was nearby.) once carried traffic across the Yuba River's South Fork. The structure, 233 feet long, is closed to traffic, but may be viewed from either end.

The weatherbeaten bridge, built by David I. Wood in 1862, has survived many storms, floods and winds, a testament to the construction methods employed by builders of that era.

Substructures were added in recent years to remove sag.

There's A Little Spot I Know

by

Jim Babcock

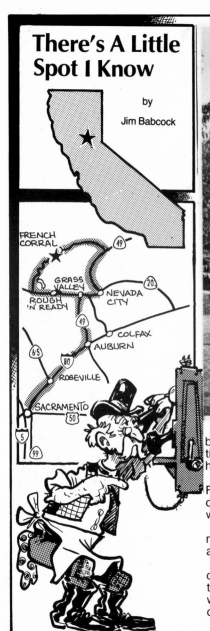

Near this spot in about 1849, a Frenchman built a corral for his pack mules. Within a short time gold miners swarmed over the surrounding hills, seeking their fortune.

The town that grew up adopted the name French Corral and it boomed, becoming second only to North San Juan in size and importance with the advent of hydraulic mining.

Today, French Corral lives mostly on its name and the one old brick building that served as the Wells Fargo Express office.

Iron doors and shuttered windows stare down an empty street. A few homes are scattered about the area, cattle roam the fields where the hotel and school once stood and the old water ditches are all but gone.

French Corral is gone, and yet it's still there.

The old town has another historic link. In 1878 the Milton Mining and Water Co. built the world's first long distance telephone line, 60 miles long, from Bowman lake to a terminous point in French Corral.

Hydraulic mining, curtailed by law Jan. 23, 1884, spelled the end to the frantic search for gold, so miners moved on and the towns dwindled like a 49er's poke on a Saturday night.

From Grass Valley, turn west on Highway 20 and watch for the turnoff a few miles past Rough and Ready. It is about 10 miles to French Corral on a narrow paved road that winds through a bit of California's history. Keep watch on the way in for the Bridgeport covered bridge — but that's another story.

There's A Little Spot I Know

by

Jim Babcock

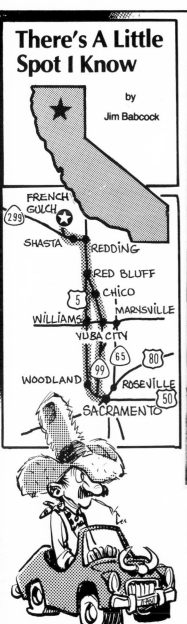

It's quiet now, not like when gold fever rumbled through the area in the middle 1800s. Then, towns sprang up overnight, boomed for a short time, and disappeared like the miners who spawned them.

But French Gulch, just west of Redding, did not disappear. It is alive and doing well. If you doubt my word, hitch up the Detroit horses and spend a delightful afternoon at this little spot.

French Gulch, nestled in the Trinity Foothills, probably received its name from the numerous Frenchmen who worked the gullies, ravines and hills during the boom years.

The old hotel, built in 1854, stands proud and tall on main street, a monument to the builder, Feeny McCampell. His grandson, Richard "Feeny" McCampbell, now retired, in the photo above stands in front of the saloon that was attached to the hotel, contemplating the many changes that have taken place in the world — but not in French Gulch.

There's A Little Spot I Know

by
Jim Babcock

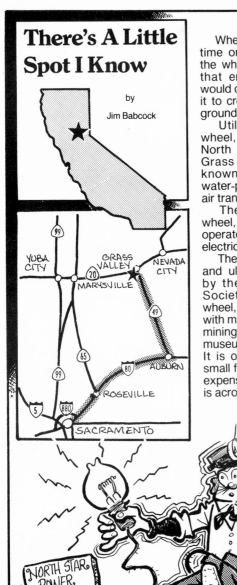

When some caveman with time on his hands invented the wheel, little did he know that engineer Allen Pelton would come along and modify it to create power for underground mines.

Utilizing Pelton's water wheel, A.D. Foote built the North Star power house in Grass Valley in 1895. It is known as the original fully water-powered compressed-air transmission plant.

The 30-foot-tall Pelton wheel, largest in the world, operated for 30 years before electric power replaced it.

The plant fell into disrepair and ultimately was rescued by the Nevada Historical Society in the 1960s. The wheel, a static display along with many artifics of the early mining days, sits in a stone museum beside Wolf Creek. It is open on weekends. A small fee is charged to defray expenses. A small picnic area is across the creek.

There's A Little Spot I Know

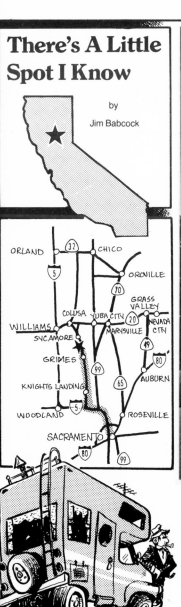

by
Jim Babcock

Don't blink your eyes as you drive along Highway E-11 between Grimes and Colusa, or you might miss the little brick shrine that sits forlornly beside the road.

In September of 1864 a visiting Jesuit priest came to this place and preached a mission to people of nearby Grand Island. A piece of land was donated for the construction of a church, and a week later, at the close of the mission, a 27-foot-tall wooden cross was erected, but no church was built.

In 1883 a Father Michael Walrath put up the shrine on this little spot. In later years the wooden cross was replaced by a concrete cross.

Occasionally a mass is held in and around the shrine — mostly around because the interior measures only about five by six feet. In the rather cramped space are a small altar, a visitors book, a crucifix and a plaque depicting the 10 commandments.

There's A Little Spot I Know

by

Jim Babcock

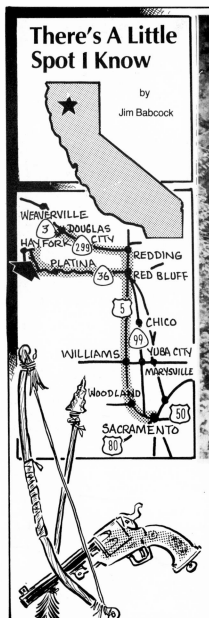

Bridge Gulch in Southern Trinity County is the scene of a massacre that brought death to more than 100 Indians of the Wintoon tribe.

The massacre, in 1852, was by whites angered because Indians had been stealing horses and robbing.

The climax came when Capt. John Anderson was slain while rounding up some of his cattle. Quickly a 70-man posse was formed by Sheriff Dixon. Trackers located the camp near the natural bridge cave at Bridge Gulch and by early morning light the shooting began. When the shooting stopped, the only Indians left alive were two small girls.

To reach Bridge Gulch, take Highway 299 West from Redding. At Douglas City turn left and follow Highway 3 toward Hayfork. Approximately 19 miles south is a sign pointing to Wildwood and Red Bluff. Turn left at the sign and proceed about three miles to the Bridge Gulch turnoff. The road to the natural bridge is one-way and unimproved. Travel about a mile on this road, then take the left branch. From this point it is a very short distance to the cavernous natural bridge that harbored a tragic event in our early California history.

There's A Little Spot I Know

by

Jim Babcock

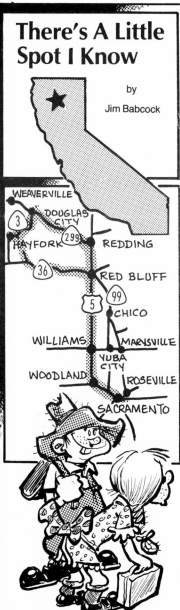

Quite a large number of Little Red School-houses are scattered around the country, but Hayfork has the distinction of having a Little Log Cabin Schoolhouse sitting right in the middle of the county park on main street.

The original school stood at Steiners Flat near Douglas City, but was destroyed by fire in the early 1920s. The replica is so authentic that only the sound of a school bell and the voices of children seem to be missing.

The school occupies a prominent spot in the Trinity County Park, surrounded by a picnic area, barbecue pits, public swimming pool, baseball diamond and a play area for small children.

To get to Hayfork, take highway 299 West from Redding to Douglas City. Turn left on Highway 3 and follow the white line over the summit and down the other side into Hayfork Valley. The park is at the west end of town.

Incidentally, don't run afoul of the law while there — the school is used as a judicial court during the week.

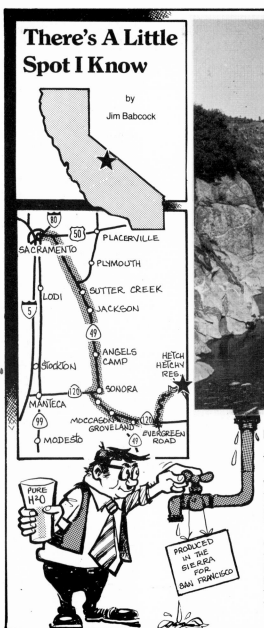

There's A Little Spot I Know

by
Jim Babcock

Somebody dammed up Yosemite National Park when I wasn't looking!

That was the impression I had on my first visit to this little spot.

Actually, this Yosemite look-alike is within the park's boundaries, but it's farther north — and it is used for a different purpose. It supplies water and power to San Francisco.

O'Shaughnessy Dam, southeast of Groveland and 16 miles off Highway 120, was started in 1913 and was completed in 1938. The dam rises to 430 feet and has a holding capacity of 360,000 acre-feet of water. Total cost to San Francisco was $10 million.

The federal government gave approv-al in 1905 to dam the Tuolumne River and flood the Hetch Hetchy Valley. Conservationist John Muir and Central Valley towns fought hard to overrule construction of the dam, but to no avail.

Hetch Hetchy, an Indian term for the grass that grew in the valley is under water, but massive granite formations rise from each side of the reservoir and resemble smaller versions of El Capitan and Sentinel Dome. In addition, Wapama Falls is a look-alike for Yosemite Falls.

Hetch Hetchy has everything that Yosemite has except most of it is under water. No public boating or camping is allowed, but the spectacular view from the top of the dam is worth the trip.

There's A Little Spot I Know

by

Jim Babcock

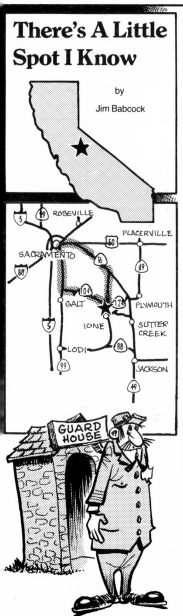

The plaque on the west side of Highway 104, just north of Ione, calls it "the most significant example of Romanesque revival architecture in the Mother Lode," and who's to argue that?

Preston Castle was built in 1894 as a center for youthful offenders who had been housed at San Quentin among older prisoners. It served until 1960 before being abandoned for newer and more modern facilities on adjoining property.

When the castle opened, seven wards of the court occupied the building along with the administrative staff and guards.

Since closing, the castle has stood its ground and watched the elements batter away until today it is only a shell.

The castle, built of local red brick and sandstone, contained 120 rooms and had 27 marble fireplaces. It housed recreation facilities, library, classrooms, cells, dorms and a swimming pool — all under the same roof.

Today the castle is a State and National Monument, but if reconstruction funds cannot be budgeted from somewhere, it may crumble and become just another "sad state of affairs."

There's A Little Spot I Know

by
Jim Babcock

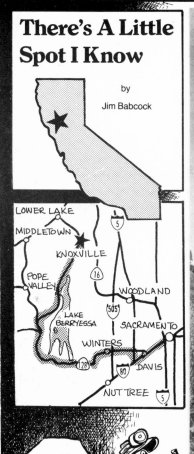

Welcome to Knoxville, Calif.

Population figures show three jackrabbits, a herd of cattle, a noisy old bluejay and a few unregistered ghosts as the only inhabitants.

That is Knoxville today, but from 1869 to 1880 more than 300 miners and their families made a living extracting quicksilver from the surrounding hills. In that period of time 61,808 flasks of quicksilver were produced.

The townspeople, miners 'n' strays all moved on, leaving only memories and the shuttered remains of the mine headquarters building to face the future.

The most interesting aspect of a visit to this remote little spot is the narrow and picturesque road that winds from the north end of Lake Berryessa to Knoxville and on to Lower Lake. That road is one of a few left in California that during the wet season have underwater bridges or creek crossings. Normally it is a nice drive, but watch for signs if you decide to make the trip during the rainy season.

There's A Little Spot I Know

by
Jim Babcock

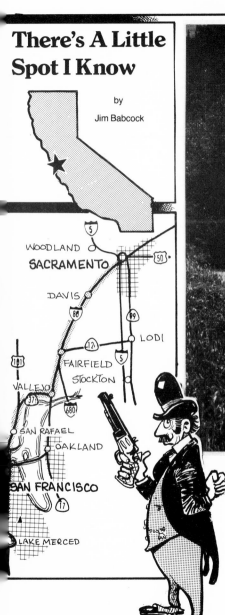

On Sept. 13, 1859, U.S. Sen. David C. Broderick and California Chief Justice of the Supreme Court David S. Terry stood at this spot, chose pistols as their weapons, walked the prescribed paces, turned and fired. Sen. Broderick sank to the ground mortally wounded.

The duel became national news and turned out to be the last one fought in California. In the history of the United States, only one other duel involving political figures was fought. That was the famous one between Burr and Hamilton.

Signs, a bronze tablet and a marble pillar mark this spot, in a secluded glen on Lake Merced's eastern edge.

In later years Terry's temper led to a confrontation with U.S. Supreme Court Justice Stephen J. Field in a railway station in Lathrop. Terry was killed by Stephen's bodyguard, David Naglee.

There's A Little Spot I Know

by

Jim Babcock

How about a little barbecue get-together? Well, this little spot has the capabilities of playing host to 999, with room for one more.

Located approximately 3 miles west of Winters on Highway 128, Lake-Solano country park encompasses 279 acres, of which 15 are well-developed for day use and camping.

The picnic area has ample tables, barbecues, toilet facilities, a play area for small children, three swiming pools and beautiful shade trèes to take the heat off on a hot day. A boat concession is nearby for those who wish to row out and try their luck at trout fishing. No boats with motors are allowed on the lake.

Across the highway is an excellent camping area, situated along the banks under a dense cover of trees. There are 50 camping sites. Facilities include toilets, showers, running water and a dump station; there are no hookups. The park is very clean, and courteous rangers are there to help and answer your questions. The price is right at $4 a night plus $1 extra for a dog.

Pack a picnic lunch and spend an enjoyable Sunday. Better still, pack a tent or R.V. and spend up to 14 days!

There's A Little Spot I Know

by

Jim Babcock

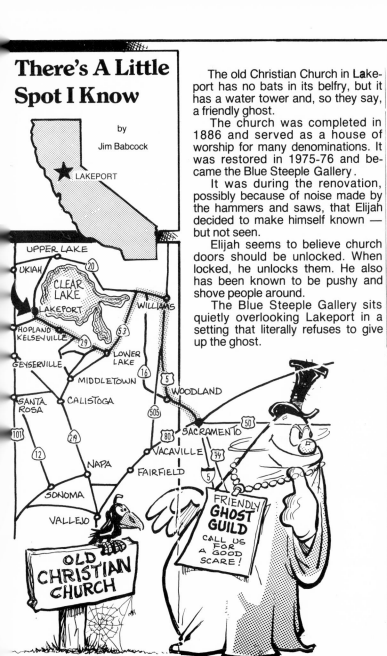

The old Christian Church in Lakeport has no bats in its belfry, but it has a water tower and, so they say, a friendly ghost.

The church was completed in 1886 and served as a house of worship for many denominations. It was restored in 1975-76 and became the Blue Steeple Gallery.

It was during the renovation, possibly because of noise made by the hammers and saws, that Elijah decided to make himself known — but not seen.

Elijah seems to believe church doors should be unlocked. When locked, he unlocks them. He also has been known to be pushy and shove people around.

The Blue Steeple Gallery sits quietly overlooking Lakeport in a setting that literally refuses to give up the ghost.

There's A Little Spot I Know

by

Jim Babcock

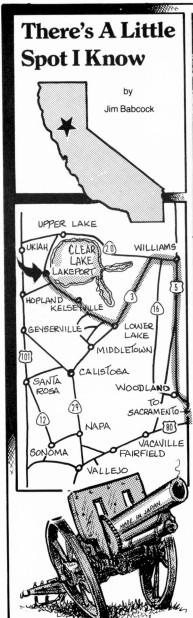

Lake County, cut from a portion of Mendocino, Sonoma, Colusa and Yolo Counties, had its ups 'n' downs trying to decide where the county seat should be located. Lakeport was the final choice, but only after four hard-fought elections, a recount and a charge of fraud.

In 1870, ground was broken and a brick two-story courthouse went up at a cost of $17,000.

A few years later the wrought-iron balcony was added so the court baliff could announce when District and Superior Courts were in session. The old courthouse was used until 1968.

The building was placed on the National Register of Historic Places on Oct. 28, 1970. It was the first courthouse in California so designated. Today the Lake County landmark houses an excellent collection of artifacts, relics and displays.

Two cannon that originally sat out front were melted down and used for brass shell casings during World War II.

Oddly enough, the replacements are imports, and if you examine them closely, you will note that they were made in Japan.

There's A Little Spot I Know

by
Jim Babcock

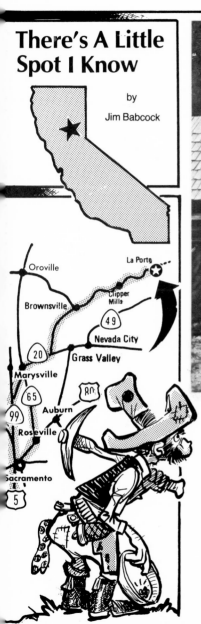

As one old timer so aptly put it, "La Porte is just too darn stubborn to quit," — even after four major fires have swept through the town.

La Porte, approximately 100 miles from Sacramento, is reached by driving to Marysville via Highway 99 or 65, taking Highway 20 east to the Browns Valley turnoff and proceeding along that road until it runs out of pavement. . . that's La Porte.

Typical small town stores dot the area, but outstanding features are along the backstreets, such as China Alley, where more than 400 Chinese lived while searching for gold along the nearby creeks; the old cemetery that dates back to 1856, and a shaded picnic area with the biggest tables that I have ever seen.

The tables, built of huge split logs, are strong enough to feed an army of people plus a zillion ants that might wander by.

Nearby is little Grass Valley Lake, loaded with fish, but I couldn't buy a book of instructions anywhere that told how to outwit them. Try it, catch a bunch and have a fish fry for lunch.

There's A Little Spot I Know

by

Jim Babcock

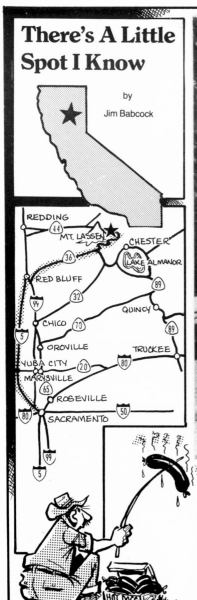

Have you ever wondered why Mount Shasta is in Siskiyou County and Mount Lassen is in Shasta County? So have I, and that brings us to the next question. Have you ever seen the little spot in Lassen Volcanic National Park known as the Hot Rock?

Many people cruising along in their air-conditioned autos and recreation vehicles zip right past the huge 300-ton chunk of lava rock that sits alongside the roadway in what was once the devastated area of the 1915 Mount Lassen eruption.

This rock is rather special, because on May 15, 1915, Mount Lassen blew its stack and started a chain of events that shoved this huge molten lava rock from the Summit Crater to its final resting spot five miles down the mountain.

The huge boulder was still hot 40 hours after the five-mile slide through mud and snow on the eastern side of Mount Lassen.

There's A Little Spot I Know

by

Jim Babcock

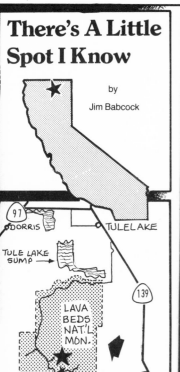

The state's population eruption is nothing compared to the volcanic eruptions that took place centuries ago in the northeastern section of what is now California.

Volcanoes in the area spewed molten basaltic lava that flowed in rivers of liquid rock.

Ultimately, the lava cooled and hardened, forming the caves and formations that make up the Lava Beds National Monument.

The park, established Nov. 21, 1925, contains about 72 square miles of interesting areas to be explored both above and below the ground.

During the summer months, park rangers give daily talks and lectures. It is suggested that visitors wear suitable clothing, including adequate headgear to protect against the low ceilings in some of the caves. It's also wise to carry more than one light source in case one light gives out. Visitors are cautioned to always check in with a ranger before wandering off on their own.

Park headquarters is 25 miles south of Tulelake off of Highway 139. Camping facilities near park headquarters are handy for those who wish to take the time to explore the more than 20 caves.

There's A Little Spot I Know

by
Jim Babcock

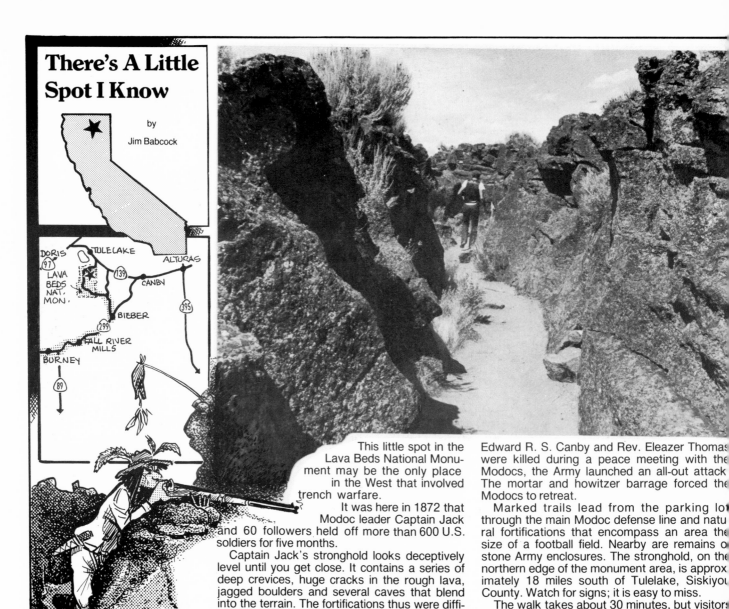

This little spot in the Lava Beds National Monument may be the only place in the West that involved trench warfare.

It was here in 1872 that Modoc leader Captain Jack and 60 followers held off more than 600 U.S. soldiers for five months.

Captain Jack's stronghold looks deceptively level until you get close. It contains a series of deep crevices, huge cracks in the rough lava, jagged boulders and several caves that blend into the terrain. The fortifications thus were difficult for the Army to attack without suffering many casualties.

On April 15, 1873, three days after Gen. Edward R. S. Canby and Rev. Eleazer Thomas were killed during a peace meeting with the Modocs, the Army launched an all-out attack. The mortar and howitzer barrage forced the Modocs to retreat.

Marked trails lead from the parking lot through the main Modoc defense line and natural fortifications that encompass an area the size of a football field. Nearby are remains of stone Army enclosures. The stronghold, on the northern edge of the monument area, is approximately 18 miles south of Tulelake, Siskiyou County. Watch for signs; it is easy to miss.

The walk takes about 30 minutes, but visitors should be sure to wear sturdy shoes and watch out for loose rocks — and a few snakes whose ancestors hung on after the fracas.

There's A Little Spot I Know

by

Jim Babcock

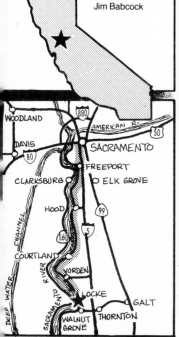

It doesn't display the usual Chinese style of architecture, but this building in Locke has had much to do with the Chinese-American students learning the culture, language and ideologies of their forefathers who settled here after the gold rush faded.

They built levees, worked the farms and ranches and settled around Walnut Grove. In 1915 a huge fire wiped out the Chinese section of Walnut Grove.

Thanks to Clay Locke, a parcel of his estate was offered to the unfortunate victims who immediately began construction of the only all-Chinese town in the United States.

The town mushroomed and soon the population topped 1,500. Sadly, today that figure stands at only 75, mostly elderly and retired.

The Joe Shoong School building originally was the Community Hall. The private school in later years was funded by the late Joe Shoong, philanthropic Chinese millionaire who founded the National Dollar Stores. The children attended day school in Walnut Grove, returned home and from 5 p.m. to 8 p.m. attended the Joe Shoong school to learn the native Cantonese language.

Today the children's laughter is missing because the younger generation moved on to the larger cities. Only the quiet sounds of the elderly can be felt and heard along the narrow streets and sidewalks — with lots of memories, but too few people to remember.

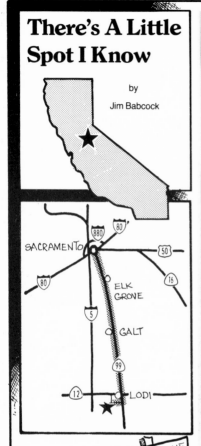

There's A Little Spot I Know

by
Jim Babcock

For a moment I thought I had died and gone to Caterpillar heaven. Not the ones that turn into beautiful butterflies, but the ones that pull plows to turn the soil.

I was at the San Joaquin County Historical Museum, just south of Lodi in the Micke Grove Park, where you also will find the zoo, Japanese gardens, swimming pool and a picnic area — a great family spot.

The collection of early Holt and Best crawl tractors is just one part of the more than 30,000 items representative of San Joaquin County's agricultural and local history that can be found at the museum. (Holt and Best later combined to produce the big yellow Cats.)

The 27 crawlers were donated by James Clack of Fresno.

The earliest model on display is the Holt five-ton, manufactured and used by the Allies in Europe during World War I. Russia, intrigued by the crawler design, reinvented the same crawler a few years later.

There's A Little Spot I Know

by
Jim Babcock

Through these arches pass the best darned people in Lodi. If you don't believe that, you'll just have to drive through and see for yourself.

The structure that welcomes you to Lodi is one of the few remaining Mission revival ceremonial arches left in California. Lodi's is one of only three left in Northern Caifornia. (The others are at Rio Linda and Winters.)

The Lodi Mission Arch was designed by architect E. B. Brown and built in 1907 during the first Tokay Carnival. It served as a symbol of agricultural and commercial growth. Except for rebuilding in 1956, the arch is essentially the same as when it was first constructed.

The next time you are tooling up or down Highway 99, take a turn down East Pine Street to South Sacramento Street, drive under the arch and get a nice, warm welcome to the City of Lodi.

There's A Little Spot I Know

by

Jim Babcock

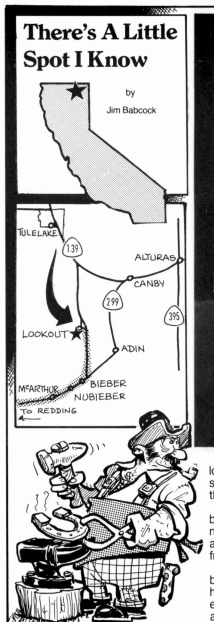

The Modoc County town of Lookout still looks out over Big Valley, possibly not with the same glint as 100 years ago, but with a spirit that hasn't dimmed.

Lookout has never been bothered by a big building boom or population explosion. That's nice, because the small town has remained as a farming and ranching area, bypassed by freeways, high-rises and neon signs.

Main street is still there, as are numerous buildings of another time. The old Grange Hall has become a grocery store with one big difference. The store and meat market are upstairs and the living quarters are downstairs. Imagine wheeling a shopping cart down the narrow stairs loaded with eggs and a watermelon?

Across the wide street stands the J.W. Leventon Blacksmith shop that has been in the family since 1888. It's all there, just like the day Joseph Leventon closed the shop in 1940. The hitching rail out front, old wagon wheels resting inside, rusty fittings and worn horseshoes tacked to the walls, even the grimy old forge sits quitely in the dark corner waiting for a breath of life from the cracked leather bellows.

The next time that you are up this way, stop and soak up some of Lookout's history. Then go away feeling a bit more down to earth.

There's A Little Spot I Know

by

Jim Babcock

Lower Lake

UPPER LAKE
CLEAR
LAKEPORT
LAKE
WILLIAMS
LOWER LAKE
MIDDLETOWN
TO WOODLAND
CALISTOGA
ST. HELENA
NAPA

This is not the little ivy-covered cottage most of us dream about.

Under that heavy foliage is the first jail constructed in Lake County.

The small stone building in Lower Lake was put up in 1885 at a cost of $200. It was constructed by Stephen Nicolai, Lower Lake's only stonemason, with two helpers, John and Theodore Copsey.

The little jail went up in jig time. Shortly thereafter, the Copsey brothers imbibed a bit too much, were ar-rested, and became the first customers of the new hoosegow.

At the time it was built the jail had the reputation of being the smallest slammer in the United States. It was so small that when the police arrested a number of Indians in 1908, six were put in the jail and two were housed in a box stall at the livery stable.

One of the prisoners had only one leg, so the authorities took away his crutch to slow him down in case he decided to make a run for it.

There's A Little Spot I Know

by

Jim Babcock

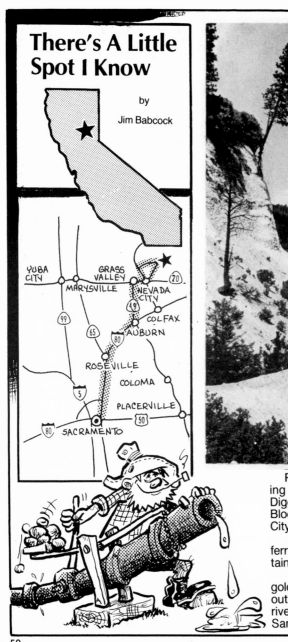

Probably the earliest form of strip mining occurred at what now is Malakoff Diggins State Historic Park near North Bloomfield, 15 miles northeast of Nevada City.

Back in the 1850s, gold miners referred to this method of removing mountains as just plain old hydraulic mining.

This way of harvesting California's gold continued until 1884, when it was outlawed due to the effect it had on the rivers, the towns in the valley and the San Francisco Bay, which was silting up.

The huge pit, where a mountain once stood, now is a 7,000-foot-long hole that is 3,000 feet wide and 600 feet deep. The bottom supports a lake.

The gold is gone, and only the scar remains. They don't make Band-Aids big enough to cover up man's greed.

The park includes restored and preserved buildings of another era in North Bloomfield. A campsite is near the townsite and visitors are invited to hike the trails that wander through this bit of California's past.

There's A Little Spot I Know

by
Jim Babcock

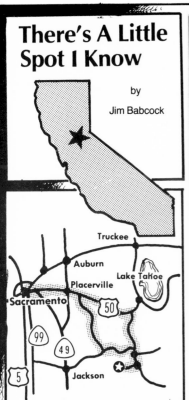

Truckee
Auburn
Lake Tahoe
Placerville
Sacramento
50
99
49
5
Jackson

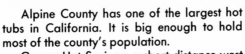

Alpine County has one of the largest hot tubs in California. It is big enough to hold most of the county's population.

Grover Hot Springs, a short distance west of Markleeville, is part of the State Park system. The park has 76 campsites with all facilities except hookups for RVs.

Grover Hot Springs is fed by six normal springs and cools from 148 degrees to a warm 102. The larger pool is a comfortable 80 degrees. Many people, seeking health benefits, return each year to bathe in the warm water.

Excess water flows into Hot Springs Creek which, incidentally, is stocked with catchables. The trick seems to be catching the catchables.

There's A Little Spot I Know

by
Jim Babcock

If Minnie or Mickey Mouse ever discovered this spot, they would abandon Disneyland and move north.

The Marin French Cheese Company, located 9 miles southwest of Petaluma on the road to Pt. Reyes Station, is noted around the world for the delicate cheeses it produces.

Since 1865, four generations of Thompsons have worked to perfect the art of the Camembert process to the point where the Rouge et Noir Camembert cheese is equal to the best of Normandy.

The factory produces other delightful cheeses, including Brie, Schloss, and Breakfast. Picnic tables are provided for patrons and tours are held between 10 a.m. and 4 p.m.

To get to the factory from Sacramento, take Highway 80 to Vallejo, 37 to Novato, turn on Novato Boulevard and go 9 miles west before turning left at the intersection.

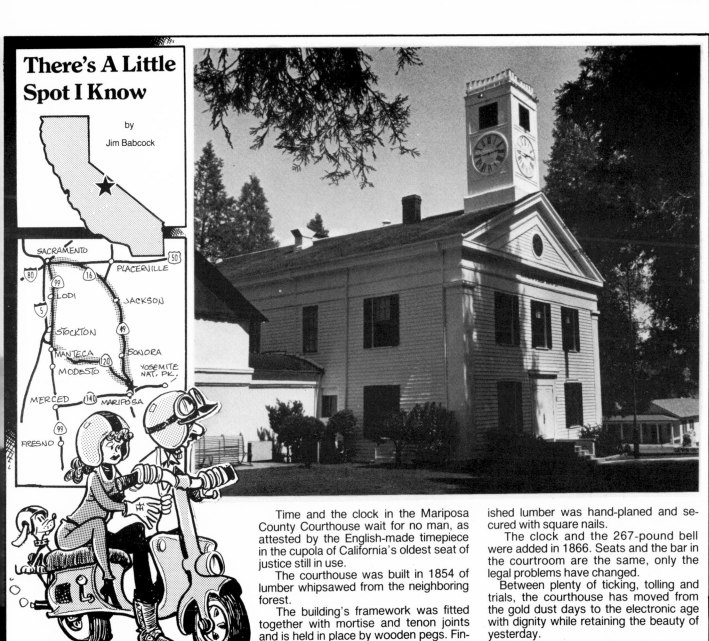

There's A Little Spot I Know

by
Jim Babcock

Time and the clock in the Mariposa County Courthouse wait for no man, as attested by the English-made timepiece in the cupola of California's oldest seat of justice still in use.

The courthouse was built in 1854 of lumber whipsawed from the neighboring forest.

The building's framework was fitted together with mortise and tenon joints and is held in place by wooden pegs. Finished lumber was hand-planed and secured with square nails.

The clock and the 267-pound bell were added in 1866. Seats and the bar in the courtroom are the same, only the legal problems have changed.

Between plenty of ticking, tolling and trials, the courthouse has moved from the gold dust days to the electronic age with dignity while retaining the beauty of yesterday.

62

There's A Little Spot I Know

by
Jim Babcock

California once boasted two towns named Marshall, one after James Marshall who dug around in a mill race at Coloma and discovered gold. The other, a small town on the edge of Tomales Bay, was named for two brothers who dug in the ground and came up with a bumper crop of potatoes.

The similarity ends there. The Marshall near Coloma eventually faded, but the one in Marin County hung on like a dungeness crab.

Marshall hangs on, seemingly held together in places by Highway 1 that winds in and out along the coves of Tomales Bay.

Today, only the Post Office, a scattering of summer homes, a boat works that seems to be working, a couple of excellent sea food eateries (closed on Mondays and sometimes on Tuesdays), and last but not least, the historical old tavern that was established in 1873.

The colorful tavern's past cannot be overlooked. It was there that rum-runners slipped in on foggy nights, unloaded through a trap door, then hustled back out to the mother ship off Point Reyes for another load of illegal booze. Then there was the time in 1906 when the San Andreas Fault shook, rattled and rolled the area so badly that the old tavern sorta slid into the bay.

The Potato Railroad and rum-runners are gone (I think), but fishing boats, dairy cattle and maybe 250 inhabitants remain. The tavern's replacement closed recently, but like the fog, I'm sure that it will return to do its thing on this spot beside Tomales Bay.

There's A Little Spot I Know

by
Jim Babcock

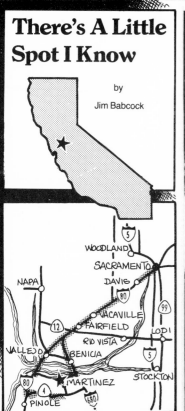

The big house on the hill in Martinez was the home of John Muir, noted conservationist, author and one of the founders of the Sierra Club.

Muir, who died in 1914, lived by his motto, "save the wilderness."

The house, built by Muir's father-in-law, Dr. John Strentzel, in 1882, became a showplace for agriculture products. After Strentzel's death in 1890, Muir, his wife and daughters Wanda and Helen moved into the home.

The brown Victorian mansion of another time is located just off Highway 4 on the edge of Martinez. The mansion is open daily to visitors for self-guided tours. Groups also take the stroll through the seven acres of orchards and vineyards. Fruits are available free in designated boxes for visitors to munch on as they enjoy the surroundings.

There's A Little Spot I Know

by

Jim Babcock

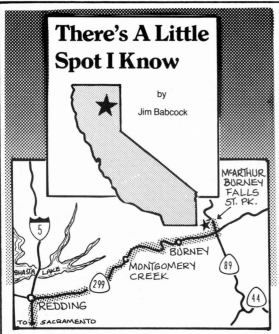

Burney Falls, near the Highways 89-299 junction 64 miles northeast of Redding, is unique. It is in one of California's oldest State parks, and bursts from an underground spring a short distance away. Summer or winter the water temperature is a constant 48 degrees.

A namesake of McArthur-Burney Falls State Park, the stream splits in two while beginning the tumble down a 129-foot cliff. Countless streams of white water gush from fern- and moss-covered areas at various heights on the face of the vertical cliff.

The park is approximately 10 miles from Burney and has 118 campsites, with tables, stoves, nearby restrooms and showers. Shaded picnic spots, nature trails, fishing and boating make this a fun place to visit.

There's A Little Spot I Know

by

Jim Babcock

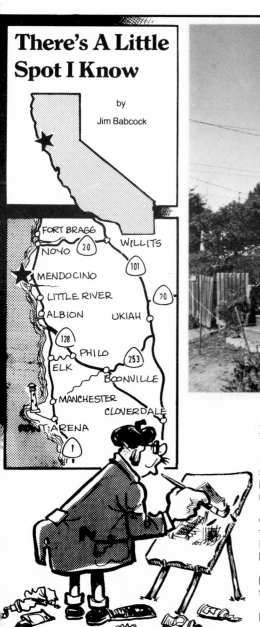

First off, this is not a Joss House, but a genuine Temple, one of only a very few in Northern California.

The temple, built sometime in the 1850s and enlarged in the 1870s, served Chinese who lived and worked in Mendocino during the heyday of the redwood lumber boom.

Mendocino supported numerous Chinese laundries, washrooms and truck gardens, but when the mill on Big River closed, most Chinese vanished like the wind.

The first Chinese to arrive in this area left China in seven junks, but only two of the vessels made it to America.

In 1852 Joe Lee landed at Caspar Beach, while the other came ashore at Monterey Bay. Joe Lee was one of the builders of the Mendocino Kwan Tai Temple.

Today, only one of the Chinese families remains in Mendocino. George Hee is deceased, but his widow, a daughter of Joe Lee, lives next door to the temple. Their daughter, Lorraine Hee, is a teacher who on special occasions will show the temple to groups.

The small red temple with the faded Chinese words over the front door sits quietly overlooking Albion Street, a fragile old building of yesteryear that faces the Pacific Ocean, which is the link to the homeland from whence those adventurous people came 130 years ago.

There's A Little Spot I Know

by
Jim Babcock

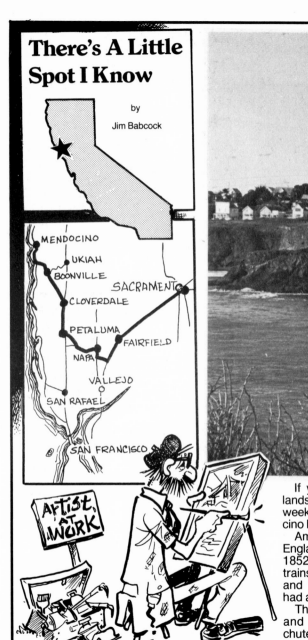

If you are looking for an interesting landscape, a colorful seascape or just a weekend escape, look no more. Mendocino has a little spot for you.

Amost a carbon copy of a small New England village, Mendocino was born in 1852 and nurtured by redwood, logging trains, a big mill on the flat, mill workers and timber baron Henry Meiggs, who had a dream.

The mill, the steam engine that huffed and puffed along Big River and the chutes that shot the lumber out to the schooners all have vanished with time, but the town remains.

The lovely old hotel, the beautiful churches, the Mendoza store, all share the narrow streets with small shops that beckon visitors. Contemporary artists and artisans in recent years have adopted Mendocino. A visit to the galleries and crafts displays makes this trip an adventure into yesterday.

A picture may still be worth a thousand words, but a visit to Mendocino is a real treat.

There's A Little Spot I Know

by
Jim Babcock

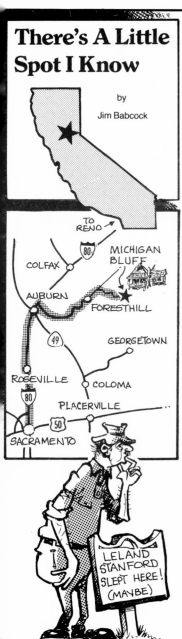

Whether the story is true or not, the trip to Michigan Bluff is a delightful ride into the past.

Michigan Bluff, with its stable population of 35 or so, sits serenely at the end of a road.

It has no service station, quick food shop or other business to mar the scene. Most homes are of another time, and each reflects the personality of its owner.

One unoccupied house today stands out as the most talked-about and controversial. The faded sign out front proclaims that it was the home of Leland Stanford when he had a tent store in Michigan Bluff. That was before he moved on to become governor.

Leland Stanford was quoted as saying that he slept on the counter in his tent store during his stay in Michigan Bluff, which sort of rules out him having a house.

Records do show that cousins of Leland Stanford lived in Michigan Bluff from 1857 and were listed by the county as merchants.

Maybe the three small cemeteries on the hill hold the answer, but no one there is talking.

From Sacramento, take Highway 80 to just east of Auburn, then turn off on the road to Foresthill. Go east four miles from Foresthill to Baker Ranch road. From there it is three miles down a narrow paved road to Michigan Bluff.

There's A Little Spot I Know

by
Jim Babcock

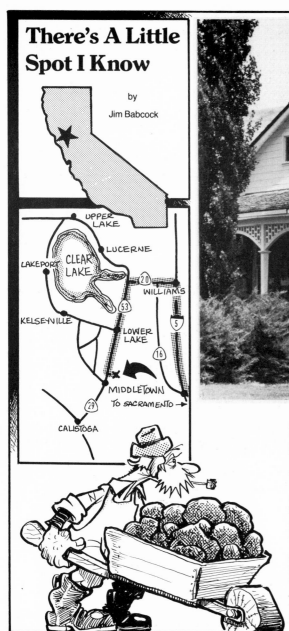

The first home occupied by white settlers in Lake County was built on this little spot, located just north of Middletown.

The original structure, a log house, was constructed by George Rock in 1850. Four years later, Capt. R. Steele and Robert Sterling constructed a stone house on the exact site. Mrs. Sterling was the first white woman to live in this part of the state.

The original stone house was built on 12-by-12 hand hewn oak logs, using oak sills and headers. The stone for the house's walls was quarried from nearby hills. The house contained three bedrooms, a kitchen and a long hallway that opened into the various rooms. It became a haven for transient families moving through the area.

In 1894, the stone house was torn down and a stone foundation was added, along with stone headers. The original stone walls were rebuilt. Total reconstruction cost was $800.

Ownership of the historical old stone house has passed through many hands, but each new owner kept it from falling into disrepair. Now owned by Hidden Valley Lake Developers, the house has been set aside as a museum and office building for the enjoyment of passersby.

It could be said that no stone was left unturned in the restoration — and that's nice.

There's A Little Spot I Know

by

Jim Babcock

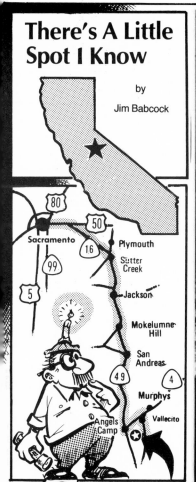

I don't know about the moaning sound, but I was panting before climbing back to the outside world after descending deep into the Moaning Cavern.

Discovered in 1881 by gold miners, Moaning Cavern was known to the Miwok Indians for many hundreds of years. Human and animal bones were found deep inside, preserved by the mineral content of the water that drips continually.

The guided tour winds down a series of narrow steps to the main chamber. From there, a steel spiral staircase, built in 1922, descends another 100 feet to an area where many historical artifacts have been discovered.

The theory that wind moving through the cavern caused the moaning sound has proved to be wrong. Actually, water dripping into natural pools give off a reverberating sound that echos through the chamber.

Moaning Cavern is east of Angels Camp, just off Highway 4 near Vallecito, approximately 85 miles southeast of Sacramento.

Group reservations may be made by calling (209) 736-2708.

There's A Little Spot I Know

by
Jim Babcock

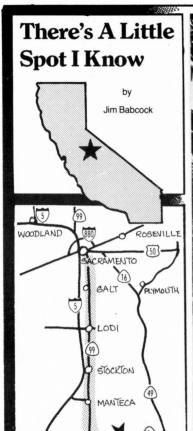

Mention Pierce Miller's name in the Modesto area and wheels start turning — mostly old buggy wheels.

Miller, a respected citizen and an aggressive agriculturalist, began his collection of horse-drawn vehicles in the early 1930s.

Soon he was into collecting early motor-driven vehicles and ultimately the early bicycles which were fabricated of wood and iron.

Today, his bike collection rivals any in the United States.

The huge red barn that sits alongside Highway 132 east of Modesto overflows with transportation modes of yesteryear.

A fire engine pumper from Santa Rosa; hose wagons from Virginia City, Nev.; an excursion bus from Sacramento; a stage coach; numerous beer, gasoline, bakery and milk wagons; and much more.

The Miller Horse and Buggy Ranch, 9 miles east of Modesto, welcomes all for a modest fee. But everything displayed is old, tired and has seen better days, so please treat this look at our past with respect.

There's A Little Spot I Know

by
Jim Babcock

Get just a pinch here and a pinch there and the first thing you know your cup runneth over with enough gold dust to build a church. Anyway, that's what they say around Mokelumne Hill.

"Moke Hill Camp" became the fastest-growing mining camp in the Mother Lode by the early 1850s. The town soon was long on stores and saloons, but short on churches.

And on that note we arrive at the Community Church on Main Street.

Back in the 1850s, like today, the good ladies of the faith were having problems coming up with money to finance construction.

Because creative financing as we know it was unheard of in those days, they resorted to hitting the local saloons and seeking donations from miners whose pokes were heavy with gold dust and nuggets.

The saloons and miners have all faded into dust, but the little white church still stands, serving the community well . . . and that's nice to know.

There's A Little Spot I Know

by

Jim Babcock

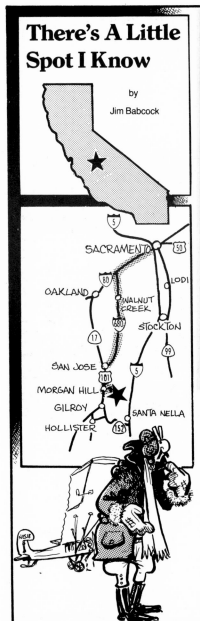

If you can remember when "dope" was used to hold fabric-covered airplanes together, then you are in for a treat when you visit the Hill Country Wagons To Wings Relic Collection on the outskirts of Morgan Hill.

Developed by Irving Perch and his wife, the collection is an outstanding display of antique and classic autos, along with some "early birds" of another day. They bring back fond memories. Crammed together, wing tip to wing tip, are the early 30s Aeroncas that looked like bathtubs, a beautiful Travel Air 4,000, an American Eagle, gull-wing Stinsons, plus a Standard biplane with seats for five and ornately painted and lettered, "The Flying Lady."

At one end of the hangar sits a huge Ford Tri-Motor that shadows a display of Austins, Cords, Hupmobiles, and even a Model T Woody. The walls are decorated with many license plates, signs and posters of another era.

Early helicopters include a one-man jet-rotor type, designed by Hiller. Also on display are the first production chopper by Sikorsky and an experimental two-man gun platform whirlybird that never really got off the ground.

It's a nice weekender. Load the family bus, yell, "clear," and set a course South on Highway 80 to 680. Continue south on 101 from San Jose to Morgan Hill. Watch for Tennant Avenue offramp, then go east to Foothill Avenue and watch for Flying Lady signs.

Not only is this an outstanding exhibit, but it is free. If you are so inclined, you may leave a contribution to your favorite charity (or) The Salvation Army. Located nearby are a golf course and the excellent Flying Lady Restaurant.

Happy Landings.

There's A Little Spot I Know

by
Jim Babcock

The narrow, twisting road that winds to the top of Mount Hamilton climbs halfway to the stars. The huge telescopes at the Lick Observatory will take you the rest of the way.

Lick Observatory, established in 1888 with funding by James Lick, was the world's first permanently occupied mountain observatory. Today it is a research station operated by the University of California, Santa Cruz.

Lick came to San Francisco in 1847, invested money wisely and in 1874, by a deed of trust, placed $700,000 in the hands of the Board of Trustees to buy land and a telescope. He made a stipulation that the telescope and observatory were to be known as the Lick Astronomical Department of the University of California.

Lick never visited the mountaintop site, high above his Santa Clara estate, but after his death, on Oct. 1, 1876, his body was carried by wagon up the mountain for entombment at the base of the 36-inch telescope. His tomb is marked by a bronze tablet that states simply, "here lies the body of James Lick."

Take Highway 80 west from Sacramento, then 680 to San Jose and take the Alum Rock turn-off. Wach for signs that say Lick Observatory, sharp turns, steep grades and narrow road in that order.

Visitors are not allowed in after sunset, so plan your day accordingly.

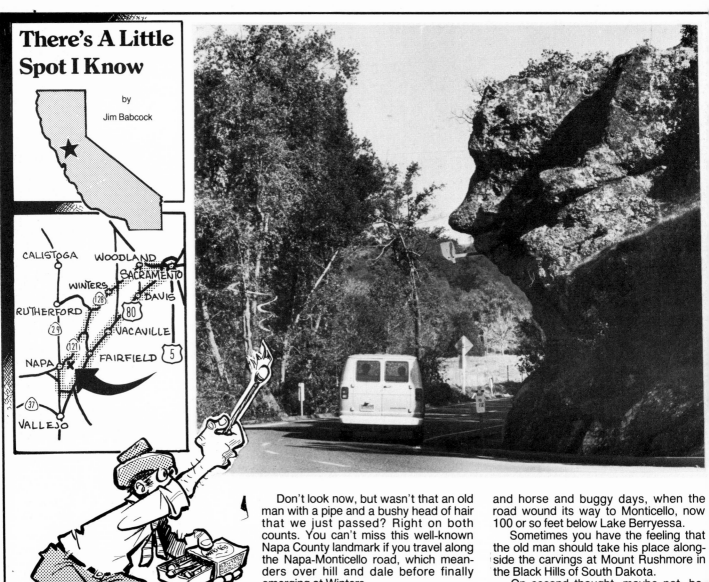

There's A Little Spot I Know

by

Jim Babcock

Don't look now, but wasn't that an old man with a pipe and a bushy head of hair that we just passed? Right on both counts. You can't miss this well-known Napa County landmark if you travel along the Napa-Monticello road, which meanders over hill and dale before finally emerging at Winters.

Located 10 miles east of Napa, the old man's metal pipe dates back to Model T and horse and buggy days, when the road wound its way to Monticello, now 100 or so feet below Lake Berryessa.

Sometimes you have the feeling that the old man should take his place alongside the carvings at Mount Rushmore in the Black Hills of South Dakota.

On second thought, maybe not, because that bushy head of hair the old man sports is real brush.

There's A Little Spot I Know

by

Jim Babcock

When one thinks of early day hydraulic mining, places such as The Malakoff Diggins, Washington, Bridgeport and North San Juan seemed to stand out, but just up the hill from Nevada City a marker locates one of the first sites where hydraulic mining was used to search for gold.

In April of 1853, at the American Hill diggings, Edward E. Matteson began using high-pressure streams of water to scour the foothills for gold.

The method used at this spot became, for a time, the standard of the mining industry throughout California and the world.

Hydraulic mining proved to be very successful, but it raised havoc with the environment.

Tailings from mines laid waste to farm lands and silted up the rivers, making it impossible for boats to navigate above Sacramento. Hydraulic mining was outlawed in 1884, after a 10-year legal battle.

There's A Little Spot I Know

by

Jim Babcock

If you look closely among the small trees and shrubs you will see one of California's very early hospitals

Located on East Broad Street at the north end of Nevada City, the huge boulder, almost completely hidden from view, was known to early pioneers as the Indian medicine stone. On top of the smooth rock are a series of hollows which Indians laid in while taking sun baths to cure their ills.

A branch of the Immigrant Trail that wound its way over the Truckee Pass and ultimately ended in the gold fields of Nevada County was located nearby.

Compared to today's modern hospital or medical center, the Indian medicine stone was rather basic. Still, the bill didn't run 500 bucks a day.

There's A Little Spot I Know

by

Jim Babcock

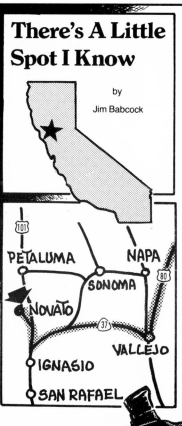

Novato, the city that mushroomed from a population of 9,000 in 1950 to a prosperous city of nearly 44,000 last year, can look with pride on its growth.

Novato is located in the north end of Marin County on Highway 101, where the city is run from a church built in 1896.

Once a farming community and later a bedroom community for San Francisco, Novato went big time in 1960, voting to become incorporated. The new city used part of its small budget to purchase and refurbish the First Presbyterian Church. When alterations were complete, on Aug. 12, 1963, government moved into the City Hall.

Just inside the front door, in what once was the church vestibule, is a donated pew from the Ursuline Novitiate of Santa Rosa. Sitting there, I had the feeling this is no place to fudge on taxes or other city business.

Located next door is the former parsonage, which now sports a Police Department sign.

The next time you are driving along Highway 101, stop in Novato and tour up to Sherman and Delong Avenues. Look for the little red church with the City Hall shingle out front. It shows you what an innovative city can do with the help of a little religion . . . amen.

There's A Little Spot I Know

by
Jim Babcock

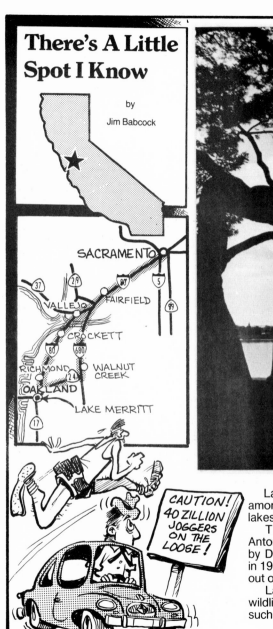

CAUTION!
40 ZILLION
JOGGERS
ON THE
LOOSE!

Lake Merritt, in downtown Oakland, is among the largest man-made saltwater lakes in the United States.

The lake, developed from the San Antonio Slough, uses a watergate created by Dr. Samuel Merritt, mayor of Oakland in 1906, to control the flow of water in and out of the lake.

Lake Merritt was designated a state wildlife refuge in 1869 and is the oldest such area in the United States. But it was not until 1909 that Oakland completed acquisition of all lake frontage and began complete development.

The 160-acre lake has a four-mile loop trail around the perimeter. Walking, jogging or just strolling leads to numerous interesting spots to enjoy. They include a children's fairyland, lakeside garden center, a Japanese tea garden, cactus garden, bird refuge, aviary and the Oakland Museum — and that's just for starters!

There's A Little Spot I Know

by

Jim Babcock

EARTHQUAKE WALK

When we talk about land movement, we normally associate it with big Real Estate deals that boggle the mind, but in the case of a little spot near Olema, in Marin County, we're talking about earth-shaking news!

In 1906 the San Andreas Fault shook, rattled and rolled, causing widespread damage throughout California.

At Olema the effects were noted mostly by terrain movement. Fences and trees moved more than 10 feet, primarily because the Pacific Plate and the Eastern Plate con-

verge at this point. Pressure between the two plates far below the surface builds up over time, setting up stresses that cause upheavals when they let go. During the 1906 upheaval the Point Reyes Penninsula moved 16.4 feet to the northwest.

Just west of Olema, Bear Valley, a part of the Point Reyes National Park offers visitors the opportunity to walk the earthquake trail and learn more of our shifting and ever-changing world.

There's A Little Spot I Know

by
Jim Babcock

Old houses come and go, but the Victorian Gothic style home that 49er Charles Fayette Lott built for his bride in 1856 lives on as a Historical Home in Oroville.

Lott family Members lived in the home until 1862, when it was deeded to the city of Oroville by Jesse Sank, husband of Cornelia Lott, daughter of Charles.

The Historical House Museum in Sank Park occupies one block, bounded by Montgomery, Third, Fourth and Bird Streets. The collection of art and historic objects included furniture, paintings, textiles, rugs, clothes, silver and glassware of the period when the Lotts lived there.

In the springtime, a walk through the Victorian Gardens is a walk through the past. Included are a rose garden, brick walks, herb garden, covered patio, gazebo and picnic area shaded by old orange trees. Throughout are numerous benches where one can stop, rest and drink in the lovely little park.

There is a small admission charge. Call (916) 533-7699 for information on visiting hours and group reservations.

There's A Little Spot I Know

by
Jim Babcock

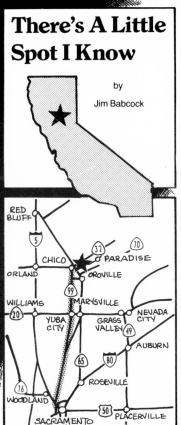

They just don't build them like they used to.

The Honey Run covered bridge, located seven miles east of Chico on the road to Paradise, proves that point quite well.

The weathered old structure looks just as good (well almost) as when it was built nearly 100 years ago by George Miller of Chico.

It is reported to be the second-longest covered bridge constructed in the state. It also has the distinction of being the only span in the United States with three different roof levels. It's expected to hold that distinction until the Golden Gate Bridge is roofed over.

Automobiles, 16-wheelers, and stage coaches are not allowed to cross the bridge but it is open to foot traffic.

Warning: If you see Ichabod Crane being chased by a headless horseman, just step aside and let them pass.

There's A Little Spot I Know

by
Jim Babcock

No, this is not just another hole in the ground, even though it may resemble a bit of mother nature's work.

This hole in the ground was created by Griffith Griffith, a native of Wales who established the granite quarry in 1864.

The quarry, located in Penryn between Roseville and Auburn on old Highway 40, once was the main industry of the area.

Granite quarried from this spot was used in the construction of many buildings in San Francisco and Sacramento, including a portion of the State Capitol. The first commercial granite polishing mill was erected here in 1874.

Griffith Quarry Park, a Placer County project, is open to the public during the week, and its small museum is open on weekends.

A walking trail, picnic tables, restrooms are located throughout the park.

If you drive Interstate 80, watch for turnoff sign near the Ground Cow Restaurant.

There's A Little Spot I Know

by
Jim Babcock

Petaluma Adobe State Historic Park might be compared to certain areas south of the border, except that the Adobe was built almost 150 years ago by Gen. Mariano Guadalupe Vallejo in the Mexican province of California.

The Adobe, built between 1836 and 1840, served as a rancho for the processing of tallow and leather which was traded to English, American and other foreign merchants.

The "Bear Flag Revolt" changed history and the rancho's period of prosperity under General Vallejo ended.

By 1857 Petaluma Rancho began to fall into disrepair and ultimately it was pretty much abandoned.

In 1910 the Petaluma NSGW purchased a portion of the rancho in an effort to preserve it. In 1951 the state took title and a long-range restoration program was put into effect. Today the building is registered as a National Historic Landmark.

Many of the rooms have been refurnished with authentic period furniture and equipment which makes a visit to this rancho an experience for young and old alike.

Take a picnic lunch and enjoy the day.

There's A Little Spot I Know

by

Jim Babcock

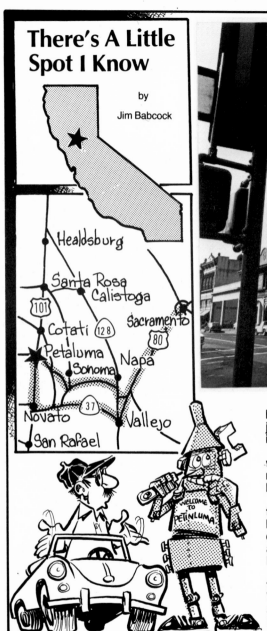

Russia is noted for the Iron Curtain, but a little spot in Northern California is just as well known for its iron-front buildings.

Petaluma, once the egg basket of the world, has in its downtown section what may be the largest collection of iron-front buildings west of the Mississippi River.

The buildings, which date from before the turn of the century, still are in excellent condition. They survived the 1906 earthquake which rocked San Francisco and Santa Rosa but did little damage in Petaluma.

The iron fronts in a sense were part of the first attempt at prefabrication in the West. They were cast in San Francisco and shipped by boat up the Petaluma River. Once on the building site the sec-

tions were bolted together and attached to the fronts of the brick or wooden structures. The facings gave the buildings the appearance of hand-carved wooden fronts with ornate mouldings, cornices and trim.

The Masonic Lodge building is seen above, crowned with the town clock. Around the corner on Western Avenue is the flamboyant Mutual Relief Building (1885) painted in purples, reds, whites and gold that makes the old buildings stand out and add to the colorful past.

To enjoy Petaluma to the fullest, pick up a walking guide at the Chamber of Commerce office on Western Avenue, then tour the downtown section and examine the architecture that flourished 100 years ago in the city's "Iron Age."

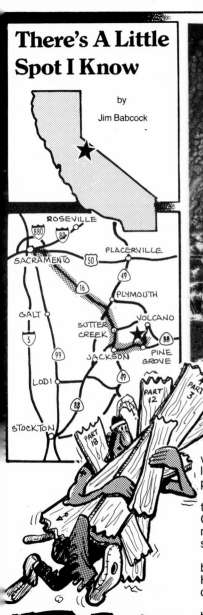

There's A Little Spot I Know

by
Jim Babcock

When we think of early Indian dwellings, we most often think of the tepee, made of tall lodge poles and covered with buffalo skins painted in colorful designs.

The Northern and Plains Indians lived in these structures, but tribes along the West Coast, lacking stands of lodgepole pine, used materials that were readily available, mainly strips of wood, bark and even tule reeds.

An example of Miwok home building may be seen at the Indian Grinding Rock State Historical Park (also called Chaw'sea), a short distance north of Pine Grove.

In addition to the Miwok dwellings the park has a large flat rock containing 1,185 chaw's-es, or mortar cups, used to pound acorns into the fine meal used as a food staple.

The park also has a roundhouse, or hun'ge, used for meetings and religious ceremonies, an Indian football field, or posco'i a we'a, and the bark-covered conical dwellings called u'ma cha'.

The park, with 21 campsites, offers Sacramentans a short weekend trip that may be enjoyed by the whole family, whether for camping or just picnicking.

To get there, take Highway 49 to Jackson, turn left on Highway 88 to Pine Grove. Turn left at Pine Grove and proceed about 1½ miles to the park entrance.

There's A Little Spot I Know

by

Jim Babcock

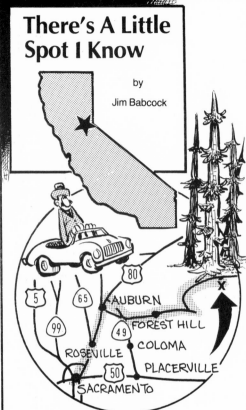

The saying, "If you've seen one tree, you've seen 'em all," is just not so.

The Placer Big Tree Grove, 35 miles east of Foresthill, includes four giant sequoias that stand out among the many Douglas fir and sugar pines in the Sierra.

The few sequoias are all that remains after a lava flow scorched the area some 2,000 years ago.

Keep your eyes peeled for the Big Tree sign as you proceed to French Meadows. The trees and picnic area are about a half mile from the main road.

There's A Little Spot I Know

by

Jim Babcock

Probably the only city in the world that boasts its very own gold mine, Placerville literally sits on a bunch of gold mines, but in this case they built a city park in, around and over one.

Two tunnels were cut into the mountain in search of the rich gold-bearing quartz vein, and were developed by William Craddock and John Dency in the 1800's, using only hand-tools, dynamite and ore cars in their quest for the big Bonanza.

Gold Bug Mine is strung with a series of lights and runs 362 feet back into the mountain. Air-shafts penetrate the tunnels, keeping the temperature at around 60 degrees. Boardwalks are covered with a thin layer of mud due to dripping of water from the ceiling. Watch your step!

The park emcompasses more than 60 acres and is bisected by a stream that meanders through the picnic area. Located across the ravine is the stamp mill, referred to as the "Peanut Crusher". A hiking trail and archery range are also within the park.

From Sacramento, take Highway 50 to Placerville, watch for Bedford Avenue and drive 1 mile north on Bedford.

There's A Little Spot I Know

by
Jim Babcock

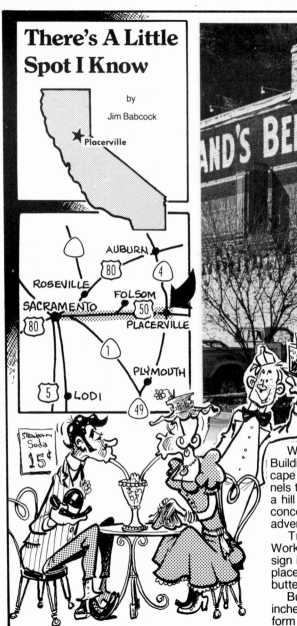

Was the John Pearson Soda Works Building in Placerville a front for an escape route though twisting mining tunnels that led from a house of ill repute on a hill in back, or was the rumored story concocted to whet the appetite of the adventuresome soul?

True or false, the Pearson Soda Works Building sits idle with a closed sign in the doorway, but once it was the place to go for soda pop, beer, ale, eggs, butter and ice.

Built in 1859, the stone walls were 22 inches thick and served as an early day form of insulation that was efficient and economical. From the Soda Works' rear a tunnel extended 150 feet back into the hill where ice and other commodities were stored. The second story, added in 1897, was used as a bottling room. A water-powered elevator was used to transport cases of bottles from one floor to another.

Snuggled up on the west side of the Soda Works is the Cedar Ravine Stables, now used as a real estate office. Who knows, maybe that was the escape route from the house on the hill. After all, they could tie up their horse and leave the motor running.

There's A Little Spot I Know

by

Jim Babcock

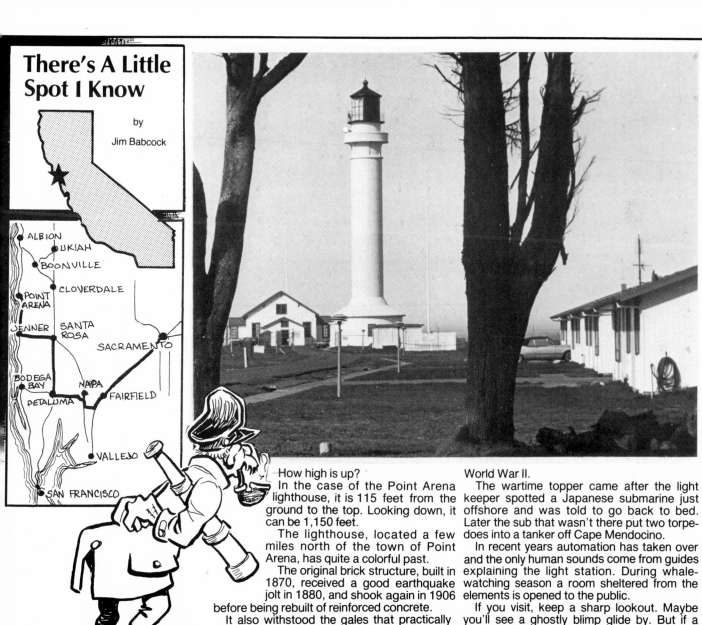

How high is up?

In the case of the Point Arena lighthouse, it is 115 feet from the ground to the top. Looking down, it can be 1,150 feet.

The lighthouse, located a few miles north of the town of Point Arena, has quite a colorful past.

The original brick structure, built in 1870, received a good earthquake jolt in 1880, and shook again in 1906 before being rebuilt of reinforced concrete.

It also withstood the gales that practically spun it around on its heavy base and it was bumped by a Navy blimp on patrol during World War II.

The wartime topper came after the light keeper spotted a Japanese submarine just offshore and was told to go back to bed. Later the sub that wasn't there put two torpedoes into a tanker off Cape Mendocino.

In recent years automation has taken over and the only human sounds come from guides explaining the light station. During whale-watching season a room sheltered from the elements is opened to the public.

If you visit, keep a sharp lookout. Maybe you'll see a ghostly blimp glide by. But if a grey whale suddenly produces a periscope, go back to bed till it passes.

There's A Little Spot I Know

by
Jim Babcock

Lighthouses were built to be seen, but in the case of the Point Cabrillo light station, the public views it from quite a distance.

It's not that there is any secret to hide, just that it has experienced some vandalism. The Coast Guard frowns on that.

On special occasions the gate is opened for whale-watchers.

The station, built in 1909 on Point Cabrillo, was strategically placed on land that juts seaward between Mendocino and Casper.

The building is one of a kind, constructed entirely of wood, rather than brick or concrete — and it is built like a brick lighthouse. Wind-driven waves have swept up the bluff hurling rocks, fish and seaweed clear up to the station door. That the station remains intact speaks well for wood!

The light was automated in the '70s and today the three homes there are occupied by Coast Guard families stationed at Noyo.

There's A Little Spot I Know

by

Jim Babcock

Point Reyes Light Station may well be the foggiest spot on the California coast.

The light station, in Marin County on headlands of the Point Reyes Penninsula, was one of the more difficult lighthouses to build. It was completed in 1870, but not before tragedy struck many times.

More than 300 steps lead down to the facility. Another series of steps take one farther down to the fog signal.

The lighthouse was made of forged iron plates that actually were bolted to the cliff. The lens, made in France, contains 24 panels and has 1,000 hand-ground prisms. The light produced a flash every five seconds.

Until 1951 the facilities were operated by the U.S. Lighthouse Service. The sta-tion was staffed by the Coast Guard from 1951 to 1975, when automation took over and the Point Reyes National Seashore assumed control.

The lighthouse is open to the public. Those with enough "go power" may hike down and tour the station that helped save many lives during the 115 years that it operated.

There's A Little Spot I Know

by
Jim Babcock

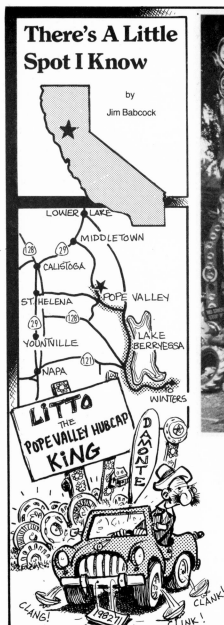

LOWER LAKE
MIDDLETOWN
128 29
CALISTOGA
ST. HELENA POPE VALLEY
29 128 LAKE BERRYESSA
YOUNTVILLE
121
NAPA TO WINTERS

LITTO THE POPE VALLEY HUBCAP KING

DAMONTE

CLANG! 19827! CLANK! CLINK!

Wouldn't you stop if you were driving along and came to a spot that has more than 3,000 hubcaps, hundreds of old license plates, highway signs of every description, odd-shaped tail lights that defy counting, and zillions of beverage can bottoms fashioned into little fans that twinkle in the sun?

Such a spot can be found north of Pope Valley on the road to Middletown. It is rather difficult to miss because the entrance stands out like a diamond in the rough.

The man behind this unusual collection is Italian-born Litto Damonte, who spent most of his life in San Francisco before retiring to Pope Valley in 1942.

The hubcap king started his collection of 'highway art' by nailing pieces to the garage in back of his home. In 40 years, his collection has grown to the point where it covers his house, patio, porch, trees, fences and outbuildings.

When you ask Litto where it will stop, he replies, "when people stop giving it to me, and I hope they never will."

He turned 90 years old in February and enjoys sharing his hobby with visitors who stop to enjoy the collection.

One other thing he has acquired in those 90 years is 39 grandchildren — and that's nice too.

There's A Little Spot I Know

by
Jim Babcock

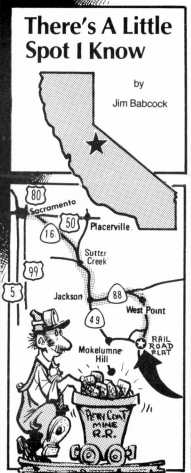

Railroad Flat was named by a group of miners who felt that they had the shortest railroad around.

The line ran a short distance inside the mine and continued to a point about 50 feet outside the entrance. The Petticoat Mine is gone, but the town lives on.

Located southeast of Mokelumne Hill, Railroad Flat no longer is a bustling mining town. Today it consists of a real estate office, Taylor Park and the country store built in 1867 by Edwin Taylor.

The 114-year-old store is owned by a descendent of Edwin Taylor. Tom Taylor and his wife lease the store, but reside in the rear of the building.

Additions have been made to the original building, including the Odd Fellows meeting hall.

From Sacramento, take Highway 49 to Jackson, turn left on Highway 88 to the West Point turnoff. Drive through West Point and watch for Railroad Flat Road. Drive slow, it's not the biggest town in the area and you might miss it.

There's A Little Spot I Know

by
Jim Babcock

Whether William B. Ide and his family ever lived at this exact spot has not been ascertained, but one thing is certain, it is well worth the time to drive the short distance from Red Bluff to see and enjoy this little spot.

The William B. Ide Historical Monument pays homage to the man who was the leader in the proclaiming of California as a republic, June 14, 1846.

Ide was born in Massachusetts in 1796, and was a carpenter and teacher before going west.

He arrived at Sutter's Fort in 1845 and later helped raise the Bear flag in Sonoma before buying the Red Bluff ranch.

He became a judge and ran a ferry across the Sacramento River at the mouth of Blue Tent Creek. Ide died at the age of 56.

The little adobe cabin and the nearby shed containing early wagons and buggies offer the traveler a chance to stop, rest and peer into California's colorful past.

There's A Little Spot I Know

by

Jim Babcock

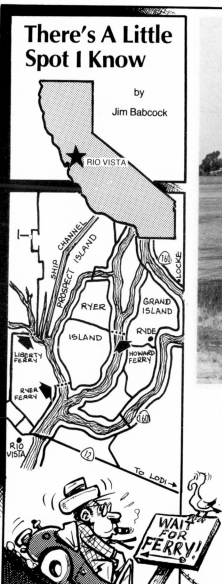

RIO VISTA

SHIP CHANNEL

PROSPECT ISLAND

160

LOCKE

RYER

ISLAND

GRAND ISLAND

RYDE

LIBERTY FERRY

HOWARD FERRY

RYER FERRY

RIO VISTA

12

160

TO LODI →

WAIT FOR FERRY!

Scooting back and forth like waterbugs on a string, the small ferries are the life line of the Delta. They are operated by both counties and state, winching themselves back and forth on an underwater cable, going nowhere, but doing an excellent job of transporting the people in the area. They serve farmers, ranchers and other produce movers as well as school children, weekend tourists and even livestock.

The Howard Island and Ryer ferries run all week long, operating from landings a short distance upstream from Rio Vista. The Liberty Island ferry runs intermittently. Other ferries, running near Stockton, include Henning Tract, Jones Tract, Venice Island, Jersey Island and Bacon Tract.

For a very pleasurable and economical weekend trip, pack the wife, kids, Grandma, Aunt Mary and anyone else who wants to tag along, then head for the Delta. It will cost only a tank of gas because, you see, the bottom line is that the ferry boat rides are free!

There's A Little Spot I Know

by

Jim Babcock

I've found a spot where the Pacific Ocean sprang a leak.

It's called the Devil's Punch Bowl, a large blow hole south of Fort Bragg in the Russian Gulch State Park.

The blow hole, located on the headlands right in the middle of a large field that overlooks the ocean, is about 100 feet across and 50 feet deep. The hole is joined to the sea by a tunnel 200 feet long. Wave action forces water through the tunnel with a great amount of power. Later the water recedes, leaving logs and other debris in the bowl, whose steep walls are lined with many varieties of wildflowers.

The huge hole is surrounded by only a rail fence, so please watch small children who might be tempted to get too close to the edge.

Russian Gulch State Park, just north of Mendocino on Highway 1, offers camping, hiking and fishing. Picnic sites overlook the headlands.

There's A Little Spot I Know

by

Jim Babcock

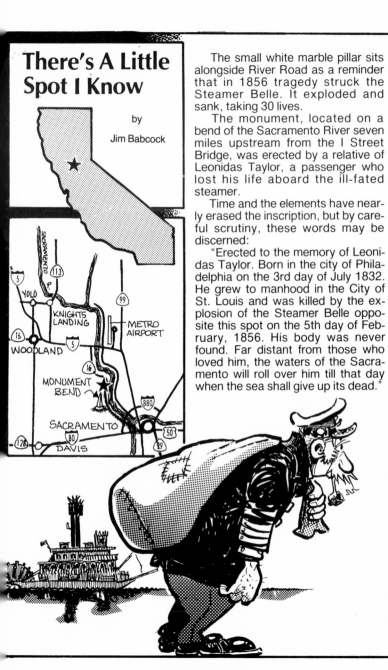

The small white marble pillar sits alongside River Road as a reminder that in 1856 tragedy struck the Steamer Belle. It exploded and sank, taking 30 lives.

The monument, located on a bend of the Sacramento River seven miles upstream from the I Street Bridge, was erected by a relative of Leonidas Taylor, a passenger who lost his life aboard the ill-fated steamer.

Time and the elements have nearly erased the inscription, but by careful scrutiny, these words may be discerned:

"Erected to the memory of Leonidas Taylor. Born in the city of Philadelphia on the 3rd day of July 1832. He grew to manhood in the City of St. Louis and was killed by the explosion of the Steamer Belle opposite this spot on the 5th day of February, 1856. His body was never found. Far distant from those who loved him, the waters of the Sacramento will roll over him till that day when the sea shall give up its dead."

There's A Little Spot I Know

by

Jim Babcock

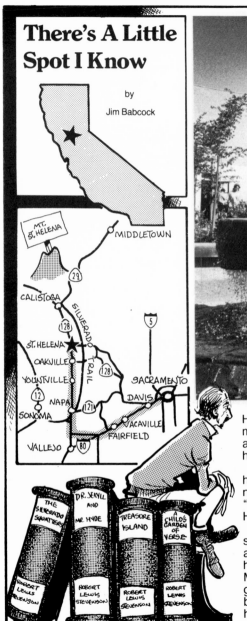

How many people can spend their honeymoon in the shadow of Mount St. Helena and then have a museum built in their honor?

Probably not too many, but that's what happened to Robert Louis Stevenson, noted author of such famous classics as "Treasure Island," "Dr. Jekyll and Mr. Hyde" and "A Child's Garden of Verses."

The museum is located in St. Helena, a short distance from where the famous author and his bride spent a two-month honeymoon in 1880 at the old Silverado Mine. It was there that Stevenson regained his health and formulated the book, "The Silverado Squatters," which he later wrote.

Thanks to Norman H. Strouse, who established a foundation to provide funds, the museum has grown from an original collection of 800 items to more than 7,500. Included are original letters, manuscripts, first editions, paintings, sculptures, photos, a collection of some lead soldiers and even Stevenson's wedding ring.

A visit to the Napa County wine country is not complete without a stop at the Silverado Museum, 1490 Library Lane, where you may turn back the pages of time and enjoy a visit with one of the great authors of all time. The museum is open from noon till 4 p.m. every day except Mondays and holidays.

There's A Little Spot I Know

by

Jim Babcock

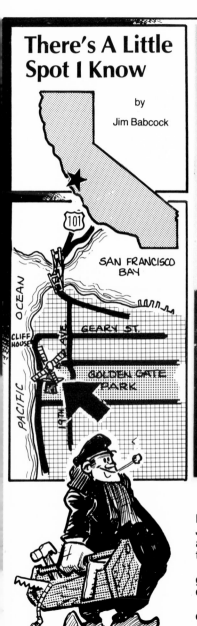

The Dutch-style windmill has been in San Francisco's Golden Gate Park for a long time. John McLaren, father of the park, built it in 1902 after he found an abundance of fresh water at the very edge of the Pacific Ocean.

He'd been looking for additional water to irrigate the west end of the large city park that extends almost to the sea.

After finding source of water, he devised an efficient method of pumping. The windmill, pat-terned after those used in Holland, served for many years before it was abandoned.

Today, thanks to generous funding and re-cent skillful rebuilding by Navy Sea Bees, the windmill stands proudly with new vanes, shin-gles and circular decking.

The beautiful and stately structure, located at the western edge of the Golden Gate Park, stands as a true landmark that John McLaren and nature built amid surrounding sand dunes.

There's A Little Spot I Know

by

Jim Babcock

Believe it or not: Enough brick was used in constructing Fort Point to build a zillion little brick houses with backyard barbecues — plus a truckload to make some gold bricks. Well, almost.

San Francisco's Golden Gate Bridge overshadows one of California's classic examples of brick seacoast forts built during the 1800s.

Erected in the general location of an early Spanish fort, Fort Point was garrisoned in 1848 by the U.S. Army. The fort was rebuilt between 1853 and 1861 and became a home away from home for 600 soldiers. It sported 126 cannons, some of which could lob shells two miles out to sea. The three-story fort boasted 30 gun rooms on each level and had walls 3½ feet thick.

The advent of the more powerful rifled cannon brought about abandonment of the old fort in 1886. It was reactivated by the Army during World War II, when soldiers there manned searchlights and rapid-fire guns.

The fort was designated the Fort Point National Historic site by the U.S. Congress Oct. 16, 1970. For guided tours and further information, call (415) 556-1693.

There's A Little Spot I Know

by

Jim Babcock

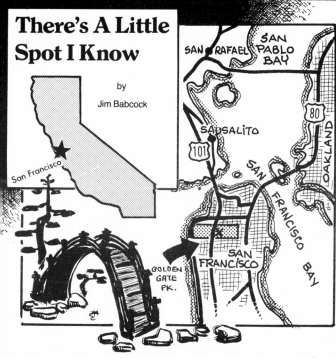

If you can't go to Japan, then bring Japan to you. The Japanese Tea Garden in San Francisco's Golden Gate Park is the best illustration of that advice.

The Tea Garden was constructed in 1893-1894 for the California Midwinter International Exposition. It flourished under the expert guidance of Makota Hagiwara and family, growing in size and beauty through the years.

Today the Tea Garden encompasses five acres. It is so well planned and executed that each step brings a new view to the visitor.

So much beauty cannot be described adequately, but must be seen to be fully enjoyed. The tall Buddhist Pagoda bounded by a Shinto Shrine fence, the large Buddha cast in 1790, the Lantern of Peace, the Zen Garden, the Moon Bridge and the quaint Tea House all are held in harmony by the walks that meander through the gardens.

Dont wait for the cherry blossom season. Go now, then return later for a walk down cherry blossom lane.

The garden is a culmination of the best efforts of man and nature.

There's A Little Spot I Know

by

Jim Babcock

RICHMOND SAN RAFAEL BRIDGE

PT. MOLATE ROAD

RICHMOND 17

TO OAKLAND 80

Once a guiding light for ships bound up San Pablo Bay to Sacramento River Ports, the East Brother Lighthouse still serves mariners, but it also serves delightful food to overnight guests and day visitors.

The picturesque light station was completed in 1874 at a cost of $30,000. It is the oldest of three wooden housekeeping lighthouses on the Pacific Coast.

It was automated in 1969. The Coast Guard abandoned the station and later it was leased and spruced up to cater to guests who want to get away from it all — but not too far away.

A charge for visitors includes a 10-minute whaleboat ride. Reservations for overnight stays must be made well in advance.

From Sacramento take Highway 80 to Richmond, then go west on Highway 17 to the Richmond-San Rafael approach. Hang a left at Point Molate road, go through the Navy Supply station and on to San Pablo Bay Yacht Club for the boat ride to the lighthouse dock.

There's A Little Spot I Know

by

Jim Babcock

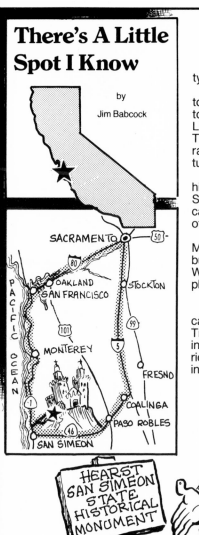

This little spot actually is a pretty big one.

Hearst Castle, or as it is known today, the San Simeon State Historical Monument, sits on Santa Lucia Mountain near San Simeon. The collection of mansions, terraced gardens, pools and sculptures can strain your imagination.

The focal point is a 137-foot-high structure that resembles a Spanish cathedral as much as a castle when viewed from the foot of the mountain.

The castle, 95 miles south of Monterey on State Route 1, was built between 1919 and 1937 by William Randolph Hearst as a place to entertain.

It is fit for a king.

Those who wish to visit the castle can obtain tickets through Ticketron outlets. The entry fee includes an extra thrill — a bus ride up the mountain via a winding, narrow road.

There's A Little Spot I Know

by

Jim Babcock

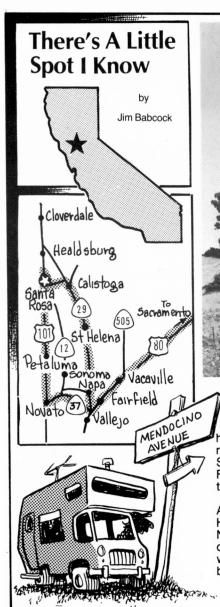

Cloverdale

Healdsburg

Calistoga

Santa Rosa

29

To Sacramento

St Helena

505

101

12

Petaluma

Sonoma
Napa

Vacaville

80

Novato 37

Fairfield

Vallejo

MENDOCINO AVENUE

What's that round red barn doing on that hillside? Strange that you ask, because that round red barn on the northern outskirts of Santa Rosa is about all that remains of the Fountain Grove Colony, which came into existence in the 1870s.

The Colony, located just off Mendocino Ave., was the brainchild of Thomas Lake Harris, primate and king of the Brotherhood of New Life. His creed and thoughts were a curious blend of oriental mysticism, socialism, with a bit of free love tossed in to keep it in balance.

The Colony originated in New York, moved to Santa Rosa in hopes of finding a new Eden at a spot they designated as Fountain Grove. Doomed to disappointment, the Colony flourished, faltered, then faded. During its reign the scandal-flecked Utopia produced some excellent wine.

Today an industrial and residential complex occupies the major portion of the site. Only the big red round barn survived the dream, that was not to be.

the
end

There's A Little Spot I Know

by

Jim Babcock

Luther Burbank put it aptly when he said, "I firmly believe, from all I have seen, that this is the chosen spot of all the earth, as far as nature is concerned. The climate is perfect . . . everything is like a beautiful spring day all the time". This chosen spot in Santa Rosa is dedicated as a perpetual memorial to Luther Burbank who contributed so much to improving fruits and vegetables.

Among Burbank's many experiments, some of the most noteworthy were the famed Burbank potato, the Shasta daisy, the spineless cactus and the white blackberry.

His method involved placing the pollen of the flower upon the stigma of another, choosing the best plant and rejecting the inferior ones. Sometimes only one was selected out of hundreds of thousands.

Luther Burbank was born in Lancaster, Mass., March 7, 1849; moved to California in 1875 and died April 11, 1926.

He is buried at the foot of a 120-foot cedar of Lebanon which he planted. At this spot he entertained his many friends and received visitors of note. The home where his wife lived until her death in 1977, the well-kept garden with examples of his work, the carriage house and the original greenhouse may be viewed and enjoyed.

From Sacrameto, take Interstate 80 Vallejo, Highway 37 to Novato, and north on Highway 101 to Santa Rosa—approximately 90 miles from Sacramento.

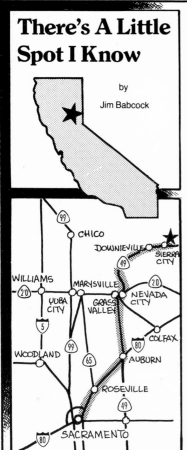

There's A Little Spot I Know

by
Jim Babcock

Want to visit a real live gold mine — with a stamp mill that thumps and bumps?

Well you can, at this spot just east of Sierra City.

The Kentucky Gold Mine is owned and operated by Sierra County, which more or less stumbled into the mining business when it bought the mill site from the Loeffler family in 1974.

Working in cooperation with the Historical Society, Sierra County rebuilt and revitalized the mill site, then added an excellent muse-um depicting the early history of the county.

Guided tours include a closeup peek into the 1,500-foot-long tunnel which extends back into the Sierra Butte Mountain. A highlight of the tour is the trip inside the stamp mill, where visitors can watch the rather crude, but effective, huge drop hammers pulverize rocks so gold can be extracted.

A small fee is charged for the tour to help meet expenses. After all, the county still hasn't made that big strike that eluded even the Loeffler family.

There's A Little Spot I Know

by

Jim Babcock

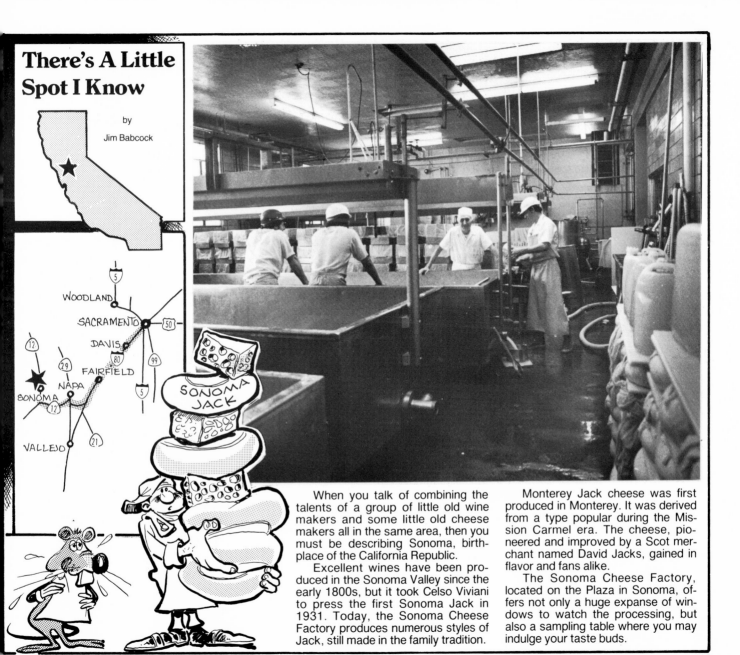

When you talk of combining the talents of a group of little old wine makers and some little old cheese makers all in the same area, then you must be describing Sonoma, birthplace of the California Republic.

Excellent wines have been produced in the Sonoma Valley since the early 1800s, but it took Celso Viviani to press the first Sonoma Jack in 1931. Today, the Sonoma Cheese Factory produces numerous styles of Jack, still made in the family tradition.

Monterey Jack cheese was first produced in Monterey. It was derived from a type popular during the Mission Carmel era. The cheese, pioneered and improved by a Scot merchant named David Jacks, gained in flavor and fans alike.

The Sonoma Cheese Factory, located on the Plaza in Sonoma, offers not only a huge expanse of windows to watch the processing, but also a sampling table where you may indulge your taste buds.

There's A Little Spot I Know

by
Jim Babcock

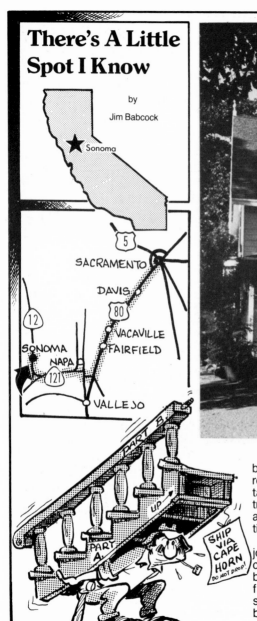

General Vallejo's home in Sonoma, built in 1851-52, features a steep pitched roof, dormer windows, carved ornamental eaves and porches to shade the entrances — typical Atlantic seaboard-style architecture that was in fashion at the time.

But that is only part of the story. Vallejo's home and one identical to it in Benicia probably were the first prefab homes built in California. Certain sections, prefabricated on the East Coast, were shipped around Cape Horn and assembled at their destinations. Redwood from a nearby forest provided much of the framing.

The storehouse, known as the "Swiss Chalet," was prefabricated in Europe. Bricks used as ballast on ships ended up in the walls as an insulation barrier. The Chalet, once used to store wines, fruits, olives and other produce, today serves as a museum, a place to store mementos of yesterday.

The museum, grounds and the home are listed as California Historical Landmark Number 4 and are open from 10 a.m. to 5 p.m. seven days a week.

There's A Little Spot I Know

by

Jim Babcock

Sonoma, site of the Bear Flag Revolt, General Vallejo's home and Sonoma Mission, has one other distinction that very few people are aware of.

In Sonoma's Mountain Cemetery is the grave of Capt. William Smith, the only veteran of the American Revolutionary War known to be buried in California.

Capt. Smith, who joined the Virginia Navy as a boy of 11 in 1779, died in Sonoma in 1846.

His grave was marked by the California State Society, Daughters of the American Revolution, on Feb. 22, 1965.

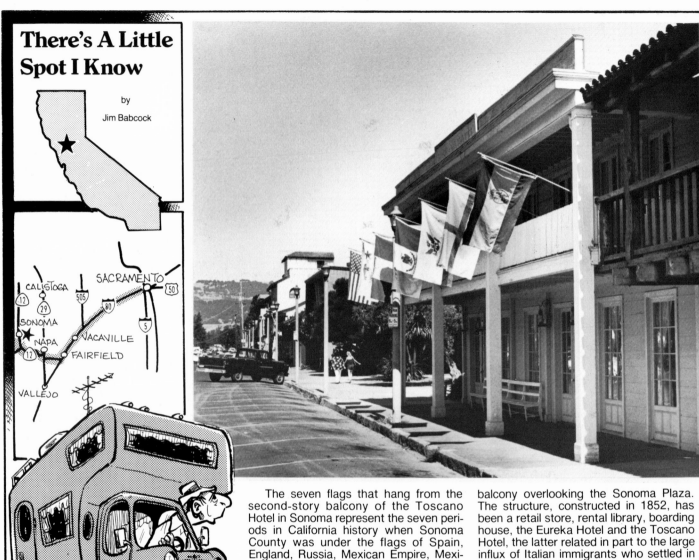

There's A Little Spot I Know

by

Jim Babcock

The seven flags that hang from the second-story balcony of the Toscano Hotel in Sonoma represent the seven periods in California history when Sonoma County was under the flags of Spain, England, Russia, Mexican Empire, Mexican Republic, California Republic and finally the United States.

Known today as the Toscano Hotel, the building served almost as many different ways as the flags hanging from the balcony overlooking the Sonoma Plaza. The structure, constructed in 1852, has been a retail store, rental library, boarding house, the Eureka Hotel and the Toscano Hotel, the latter related in part to the large influx of Italian immigrants who settled in the area.

Toscano Hotel started as the Tuscano, but that doesn't alter the historical significance of the 131-year-old building that peers out from behind the seven flags.

There's A Little Spot I Know

by
Jim Babcock

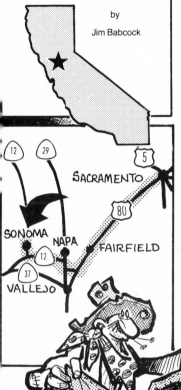

This spot in Sonoma became the scene of the Historical Bear Flag Revolt. General Vallejo was taken prisoner by 33 Americans on June 14, 1846, the Mexican Flag was pulled down and the flag of the Republic of California was raised. The homemade flag, which bore a star and a grizzly bear, was unfurled and flew until it was replaced by the United States flag on July 9, 1846. Sonoma Plaza, largest plaza in California, is surrounded by numerous historical buildings, including San Francisco Solano Mission, Sonoma Barracks and the site of Vallejo's Casa Grande.

There's A Little Spot I Know

by
Jim Babcock

Maybe this massive rock is not as immense as the Rock of Gibraltar, but it is quite impressive to see as you motor north up the Redwood Highway.

Squaw Rock rises high above the Russian River along Highway 101, just 6 miles south of Hopland in Mendocino County.

Indian legend tells that a beautiful maiden named Sotuka was in love with a faithless lover, Chief Cachow, who married another.

Sotuka, unable to control her emotions, climbed to the top of the 500-foot-tall rock. While the chief and his wife slept at the base, Sotuka, holding a huge rock, jumped from the top, landing on the two and killing them.

The legend doesn't say, but we may assume the sudden stop brought an end to Sotuka as well as the lovers.

A large parking area assures the motorist a spot to stop and rest at the base of Squaw Rock.

There's A Little Spot I Know

by

Jim Babcock

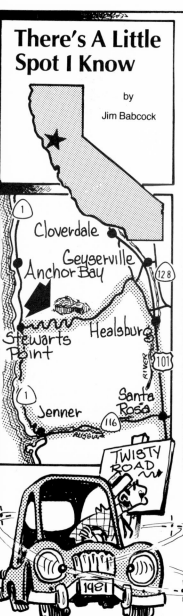

Some people refer to these unusual structures as round houses. Others call them meeting houses, even sweat houses, but no matter what you may call them, they are a major part of California's Indian history.

Four miles from Stewarts Point, on the twisty road that ultimately winds up in Healdsburg, is the small Kashia Indian Reservation. There, a short distance down a dirt street, is the old redwood roundhouse where the Indians met to work out problems, hold ceremonial dances and delve into the mysteries of life.

The structure, built primarily of rough sawn boards, with a shake roof and supported by huge poles, now stands alone. It has been replaced by a modern structure, but time should not destroy this little spot in our California history.

If you decide to visit, drive with caution. The road, though paved, is crooked and has numerous blind turns.

There's A Little Spot I Know

by
Jim Babcock

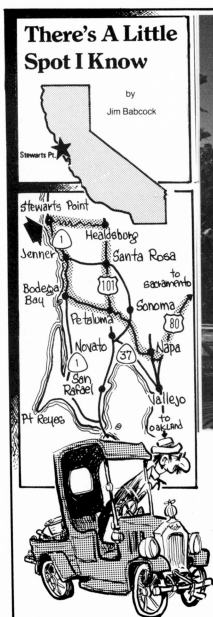

Stores come and go, but the crackerbox-style general store at Stewarts Point may go on forever. The store, built in 1868, probably was a forerunner of today's supermarkets. The ground floor held a section of groceries, dry goods, meat market and confections needed to supply the local inhabitants. In early days the Post Office occupied part of the store.

But upstairs was where things happened on Saturday nights. Dancers do-si-doed to the music of four or five musicians all night long, often until it was time to go and milk the cows on Sunday morning.

The porch in front of the store normally was occupied on Sundays by the Kashia Indians from the reservation located a few miles east of Stewarts Point. Dressed in their finest and whitest shirts and wearing new blue overalls, the Indians would walk or ride buggies on down to sit and watch the passing parade.

Until the roads were improved, Stewarts Point was isolated and depended on the coastal schooners that carried lumber and supplies up and down the coast.

The Richardson family has owned and operated the historical old store since 1881. The old kerosene can with the potato on the spout is gone, as are the 50-gallon barrels that dispensed gasoline at 20 cents a gallon, but it is still Stewarts Point store and that's nice.

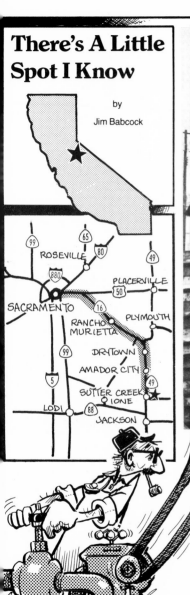

From the exterior, the structures look like any other three small, corrugated-steel buildings, but what goes on inside is unique in the United States.

The 109-year-old foundry-machine shop in Sutter Creek uses only water power to operate its metal-turning lathes, grinders, drills, planers and air compressors.

The foundry, begun by Samuel N. Knight and George Horne, operates in the same manner as when it started in 1873.

Instead of turning out water wheels and gold-dredging hoists as in the past, though, the present owner, Carl Borgh, turns on the faucets and produces custom castings for customers throughout the world.

Water flows from the Sierra watershed into Pacific Gas & Electric Co.'s Tanner Reservoir, where it is diverted into a holding pond. From the pond the water drops 500 feet through a 10-inch pipe to the foundry.

Gravity causes the water to build up a pressure of 200 pounds per square inch before it enters the water turbines which drive belts that operate the machinery.

After passing through the turbines the water flows downstream to Ione, where it is used for drinking water.

In the foundry, casting normally is done on Fridays. Then, it is possible to stand near the open doorway and watch work being done just like it was 100 years ago.

There's A Little Spot I Know

by

Jim Babcock

Trinidad Head is almost, but not quite, an island. Connected to the mainland by a short strand of beach, the head protects the harbor from winds that snarl out of the north. Once a large whaling station and port for the small freighters that plied the coast, Trinidad is considered one of the most picturesque harbors along the coast.

The brick lighthouse, located on the steep side of the Trinidad Head, was completed in 1871. A narrow road led across the spit and snaked its way up the head. Because of its size the lighthouse rated only a fourth-order beacon.

In 1898 a fog signal was installed and from that time on a two-ton bronze bell guided ships and fishing vessels back to the harbor during inclement weather.

Automation took over in the early 1970s, when the old light was removed and placed in a small park that overlooks the harbor. The old bronze bell, a life saver in its own time, was placed next to the light.

There's A Little Spot I Know

by
Jim Babcock

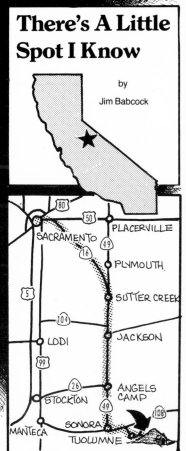

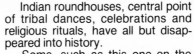

Indian roundhouses, central point of tribal dances, celebrations and religious rituals, have all but disappeared into history.

Some, such as this one on the Tuolumne Reservation, seem to be sinking into the ground. That, however, is not the case — they were built that way.

In California, no more than a dozen of the original roundhouses still stand. Most have been replaced by modern tribal centers that func-

tion as administrative offices and meeting areas for reservation dwellers.

Each year in September the Tuolumne Reservation holds a two-day fete during which the public is invited to enjoy the dances and games.

From Sonora, take Highway 108 to the Tuolumne turnoff. Continue through the town of Tuolumne for approximately one mile to the paved road that leads you to the reservation.

There's A Little Spot I Know

by
Jim Babcock

It's definitely not Washington, D.C. or Washington State, but Nevada County's town of Washington has its own personality and character that will match the others.

Approximately 14 miles east of Nevada City on Highway 20 is the turn-off. This develops into a series of squiggly turns that don't stop until they reach the South Yuba River at the bottom of the canyon.

Once a roaring gold mine town, Washington has become a retirement spot and a place to get away from it all.

Washington's claim to fame might be that there were more bars up and down the river than any other spot in California. Included would be the Canal Bar, Long Bar, Keno Bar, Jimmy Brown's Bar, Boulder Bar, Rocky Bar, Brass Bar and last but not least, Whisker Bar.

Today the town has only a general store, post office, hotel, restaurant, trailer park and neat little park with one barbecue, a table, two trees and a flag pole. Arrive early if you want to get a seat.

There's A Little Spot I Know

by

Jim Babcock

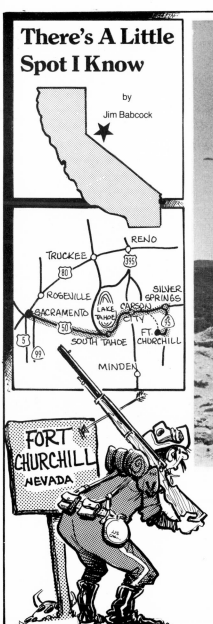

OFFICERS QUARTERS

KEEP OUT OF RUINS

Fort Churchill State Park in Nevada can be reached in two ways.

The best way is via Highway 50 east about 40 miles from Carson City. At Silver Springs, turn right on Alternate 95 and follow the paved road to the entrance of the park.

The more scenic route leaves Highway 50 just east of Dayton. That bumpy dirt-and-gravel washboard goes for 16 miles before finally winding up at the Fort. Ignore that sign by the bad road and wait for the good one.

Fort Churchill was built in 1860 in an effort to quell disputes and fighting between the Indians and white settlers of the area. For nine years the Fort guarded the Pony Express, ranchers, depot supplies and acted as an early day "buffer zone."

The fort was abandoned in 1869 and was sold at an auction for only $750. Today, the fort includes an information center, a 20-unit campground, a picnic area along the Carson River and the numerous old stone buildings that seem to stand in defiance of man and the elements.

There's A Little Spot I Know

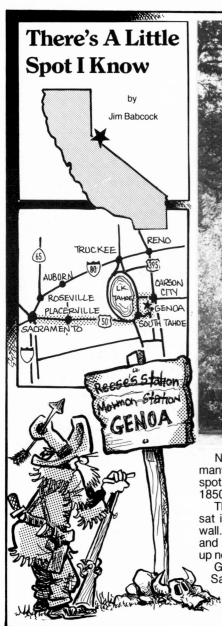

by
Jim Babcock

No, Abraham Lincoln did not sleep here, but many tired, weary, thirsty immigrants found this spot on their trek to Golden California between 1850 and 1868.

The original structure, a log-walled building, sat in an area surrounded by a high stockade wall. John Reese soon added a blacksmith shop and stable. Soon a flour mill and sawmill went up nearby.

Genoa was the only permanent link between Salt Lake City and California; the first permanent settlement in the State of Nevada. The original station, with its much higher stockade wall, burned in 1910. A replica was built on the exact spot in 1947.

Today the small community sits quietly on the eastern slope of the Sierra. There's the beautiful old weathered courthouse that once served Carson County and is now a museum. Up the street is the oldest bar in Nevada, bottled up with memories, and there is the Mormon Station and its museum. With shade trees, a green lawn, picnic tables and barbecues, Genoa is like an oasis on the edge of time.

From Sacramento, take Highway 50 to South Lake Tahoe, turn right on Kingsbury grade, wind up and over. Watch for the left turnoff to Genoa at the base of the mountain.

There's A Little Spot I Know

by

Jim Babcock

The first impression I had upon seeing the Bottle House in the ghost town of Rhyolite was that the builder must have had a fantastic hangover when he finished construction.

Rhyolite's is considered the most famous of the mining camp "bottle houses." The building, which contains 50,000 bottles of assorted sizes, was completed by Tom Kelly in February of 1906.

The house fell into disrepair and was restored in 1925, using the original bottle walls.

The late 1800s boomer is a must for tourists interested in Nevada's early mining towns — a quiet place where camera-laden tourists drudge its streets looking for picture angles and locals seek a new angle on life.

There's A Little Spot I Know

by

Jim Babcock

Virginia City, Nev., boomed for 20 years after the discovery of gold and silver in 1859.

Today the old town booms with tourists intent on spending their money for souvenirs, cowboy hats, personalized T-shirts and dropping a few bucks in the one-armed bandits that clang in watering holes along the main drag.

During the heyday of silver and gold mining, more than $400 million was re-moved from seven major mines in, around and under the town. The Sierra Nevada, the Union, Ophir and Con Virginia mines combined to help bring Nevada into the Union and to build San Francisco.

If all of the modern modes of transportation suddenly disappeared, you could step back 130 years in time as you walk the boardwalks past the many stores, opera house, and homes that speak of another time.